Mediocre Me

Mediocre

How Saying No to the Status Quo
Will Propel You From
Ordinary to Extraordinary

Me

John E. Michel

Brigadier General, USAF

<small>NEW YORK</small>

Mediocre Me

How Saying No to the Status Quo Will Propel You From Ordinary to Extraordinary

ISBN 978-1-61448-440-0 paperback
ISBN 978-1-61448-441-7 eBook
Library of Congress Control Number: 2012951506

Morgan James Publishing
The Entrepreneurial Publisher
5 Penn Plaza, 23rd Floor,
New York City, New York 10001
(212) 655-5470 office • (516) 908-4496 fax
www.MorganJamesPublishing.com

Cover Design by:
Rachel Lopez
www.r2cdesign.com

Interior Design by:
Bonnie Bushman
bonnie@caboodlegraphics.com

In an effort to support local communities, raise awareness and funds, Morgan James Publishing donates a percentage of all book sales for the life of each book to Habitat for Humanity Peninsula and Greater Williamsburg.

Get involved today, visit
www.MorganJamesBuilds.com.

Habitat
for Humanity®
Peninsula and
Greater Williamsburg
Building Partner

Dedication

This book is dedicated to all those citizens in the world who are leading the change they want to see. In honor of your selfless example, it is my great privilege to donate the majority of net profits from the sale of this book to a series of charity organizations serving our nation's military members and their families. These include:

The Wounded Warrior Progam; The Air Force Aid Society; Fisher House Foundation; the Intrepid Fallen Heroes Fund; and Supporting All Veterans Equally (SAVE).

Consider *Mediocre Me* to be my small way of saying thank you to all those in our midst who are making our nation and our planet a better and brighter place to live, work, play, and pray, each and every day.

In service,
John E. Michel
Brigadier General, United States Air Force

Contents

Prologue: The Legend of the Willing Burden Bearer   *ix*

Introduction: Don't Ignore Warnings   *xv*

Part One: Redefining our Boundary Markers

Chapter 1: The Mess We're In   3

Chapter 2: Sparks of Positive Change   13

Chapter 3: Invisible in Plain Sight   23

Chapter 4: Make Different, More Empowering Choices   31

Part Two: The Choices: Transforming Good Intentions Into Deliberate Attitudes & Actions

What If?   **41**

The First Choice: Take Risks...Be Proactive   **45**

Chapter 5: Be the First Penguin   47

Chapter 6: Risk Going First   55

The Second Choice: Model the Change You Want to See...Be Responsible   **65**

Chapter 7: Be the Difference You Want to See   67

Chapter 8: Reclaim Responsibility   76

The Third Choice: Love thy Neighbor...Be Compassionate   **87**
Chapter 9: Practice Jen   89
Chapter 10: Suffer With Affection   97

The Fourth Choice: Fight for What's Right...Be Truthful   **107**
Chapter 11: Be Willing to Give It All   109
Chapter 12: Live Your Truth   119

The Fifth Choice: Embrace Change...Be Hopeful   **129**
Chapter 13: Facing Your Fear of Change   131
Chapter 14: Make Hope a Habit   142

The Sixth Choice: Check Your Ego...Be Grateful   **153**
Chapter 15: Beware the Ego Trap   155
Chapter 16: Practice Thankfulness   165

The Final Choice: Make Your Character Count...Be Real   **175**
Chapter 17: Character: Coin of the Realm   177
Chapter 18: Don't Chunk!   185
Conclusion: Lead Your Life for a Higher Purpose   193

Epilogue: Dream Big Dreams   *198*
www.secondmilesolution.com   *203*
Notes, Cautions & Warnings Summary   *205*
Acknowledgments   *211*
About the Author   *213*
Endnotes   *215*

The Legend of the Willing Burden Bearer

Life begins at the end of your comfort zone.
—Neale Donald Walsch

On a dusty road in a field in ancient Israel, three teenage boys walk together, enjoying each other's company. It's a beautiful spring morning marked by a cloudless, blazing blue sky. A perfect setting for friends to relish the promise of a day filled with laughter, stories, and a shared meal.

However, as the young men turn down a familiar path, they encounter a Roman soldier returning from guarding a local outpost. Aware of the law of the land enabling those with formal power and authority to compel non-Roman citizens to carry their heavy loads for up to a mile, the boys momentarily consider bolting from the scene.

But they quickly realize fleeing is futile.

Going the first mile is compulsory.

Instinctively, the Roman centurion barks out the anticipated order— "Come here!"—motioning for one of the teenagers to join him. Two of the *young men step back, but the third, Joshua, willingly steps up. "Take my pack," the soldier demands, and, despite the rucksack being almost a hundred pounds, the citizen complies. After all, he's quite familiar with the law, as it's not the first time he's been asked to bear another's burden.*

And he knew it would not be his last.

Setting out down the dusty road before them, the minutes pass in silence. The Roman centurion, weary from months away from his family and a string of border skirmishes that left him physically bruised and mentally exhausted, is enjoying this brief moment of rest. His hardened, gruff exterior masks the heart of a man who would rather be home tending to the family's farm than fighting a nation's wars in distant, far-away places.

In what seems but a matter of seconds to the tired soldier, the familiar mile marker comes into view. At the designated spot, he stops, ready to reclaim his load. After all, the minimum requirement had been met. The young man had complied and was now free to move on.

But to the soldier's surprise, the citizen chooses to keep going.

Without saying a word, this burden bearer continues down the dusty road before him in the direction of the next mile marker.

No frown.

No fret.

No fanfare.

Leaving the soldier to question what compelled this particular citizen to willingly deviate from the status quo and risk walking differently in the world.

Who doesn't love a good legend? The fountain of youth, Robin Hood, King Arthur, and the Holy Grail are but a few that most frequently come to mind. But have you ever paused to think about what makes legends so appealing?

For one, legends are historical stories that capture our attention. Unlike a myth, which focuses on explaining natural phenomena by addressing why things are the way they are in the natural world, a legend often focuses on individuals and their accomplishments or on items with transformative potential. In many cases, the heroes or objects of legends reflect something we deeply admire, wish we possessed ourselves, or help us focus on timeless lessons we'd be wise to learn or relearn.

For example, the fountain of youth is appealing because its waters promise the restoration of youth and vitality. We love what Robin Hood represents because his lifestyle and his actions speak of the nobility in fighting against injustice and tyranny. The legendary British leader King Arthur provides us with a compelling example of what it means to lead a life of courage, integrity, and selfless service. And the Holy Grail—well, that may just be the greatest legend of them all, promising miraculous powers to anyone who can claim it as their own.

Taken together then, legends transcend culture, doctrine, and philosophy by pointing our imaginations toward the realm of the possible. They represent stories, true or otherwise, which live on from generation to generation because they captivate our thoughts and quicken our hearts, providing common ground we can use to explore those timeless values, principles and ideals we believe are worth preserving and maybe even one day emulating ourselves.

One of the other reasons we are so drawn to legends is that they give us a glimpse of what it means to lead our lives in a more excellent way. What specifically do I mean by this statement, you ask? It's simple. It begins by recognizing that the quality of our life is determined largely by the quality of our thoughts. Think small, live small. Choose to be average and the one thing that's virtually guaranteed is that we will achieve our goal every time.

However, if we expand our view of the potential role we can play in the world, everything changes. Instead of taking the path of least resistance and accepting the status quo is something we can't influence, committing to leading our lives in a more excellent way demonstrates we are willing to take a very different approach. An approach that provokes, conspires, and inspires us to consistently push the bounds of our abilities and stretch the full extent of our capabilities so we can live a life of true purpose, meaning, and significance.

Surveys confirm that the desire to achieve something meaningful and significant in and through our lives is important. In fact, reams of research affirms millions of us – more than three out of every four adults – say we are interested in making a positive difference in the world. We want to become the best version of ourselves and have our lives characterized by such terms as relevant, significant, and dare I say, *excellent*.

Psychologists actually have a name for this built-in desire to become the best version of ourselves. It's called *actualizing tendency* and derives from the belief we all possess a built-in motivation to grow, to develop, and to enhance our individual and collective capacities. Through such a lens then, we are viewed as leading our lives in a more excellent way anytime we are *doing something* productive to stretch our horizons, expand our boundaries, and build value into our surroundings.

But if excellence is one of our primary aims in life, why is it we so often find ourselves missing the mark? How is it that an attitude of "good enough," what I term a *mediocre me mindset*, so frequently or conveniently becomes a suitable alternative to giving our best to build an excellent company, or be an excellent spouse, sibling, parent, politician, soldier, athlete, and on and on?

When did mediocrity, the sad state of affairs that strives to shrink our imaginations, dim our dreams, and diminish our potential, become such a suitable alternative to striving to lead our lives in a more excellent way each day in a multitude of ways? The answer: the moment we allowed it to.

What might the symptoms of having accepted a *Mediocre Me* mindset look like in your life? Take a moment to reflect on the following questions:

Do you find yourself frequently doing just enough to get by?

Do you often wonder if this is all there is in life?

Do you resist opportunities to change, even when you know doing so is the right decision?

Are words like "it's not my fault" a frequent part of your vocabulary?

Do you have a difficult time recalling the last time you tried something new?

Does every day feel like ground hog day?

If more than a couple of these statements hit close to home then you may very likely be stuck. An unwitting prisoner of mediocrity that denies its own existence as it enshrouds us in a false sense of comfort and security—ultimately persuading us to adopt a way of thinking and being in the world that convinces us settling to be average is an acceptable way to lead our lives.

Of course, there may be some reading this wondering if mediocrity is really such a bad thing? After all, it's certainly easier, safer and more comfortable to continue to do what we are most familiar with. But here's the rub with this line of reasoning. Although there are certainly times when settling for mediocrity may make sense, consistently choosing to operate below our potential by allowing average to become our preferred response starts us down a path of compromise in which most of us will never return. I suspect this is what Jim Collins was referring to when he shared in his landmark book, *Good to Great,* how the only way we will discover and sustain excellence in and through our lives is if we continually highlight its significance. "Good is the enemy of great," he writes. "And that is one of the key reasons why we have so little that becomes great."

For almost two thousand years, the legend of the willing burden bearer has captured the attention of people across the globe. The story of a common citizen with no formal power, authority, rank, or title, who *chose to say no to the status quo*—one person who defied expectation without explanation, his counterintuitive move leaving us to question the source of his motivation as to why he chose to walk differently in the world.

As you'll discover for yourself shortly, this timeless legend reveals how overcoming mediocrity and embracing excellence is much simpler and straightforward than one might expect. In fact, you may be surprised to find it's largely a matter of committing to making different, more empowering *choices* in how you routinely interact with those in your sphere of influence—choices which can transform ordinary encounters into extraordinary opportunities to guide, inspire, and be helpful in a way that willfully does for others what you would like others to do for you by setting an example worth emulating.

Too often, we allow mediocrity to creep into our lives which conditions us to lower our sights and dilute our standards. Blinding us in the process to the reality that learning to lead our lives in a more excellent way has little to nothing to do with formal education; degrees don't confer excellence. It has nothing to do with how wealthy we are; money doesn't buy us excellence. Nor is it about having friends in high places; position doesn't equate to excellence. Excellence then is best measured by how we *choose* to use the opportunities we have every day to have more impact, make more of a difference, and lead a life of true purpose, meaning, and significance.

Remember, it's easy to be average. You know it. I know it. Mediocrity is simply a choice we make every day. If we feel like we're running in place, there is a good chance we are tolerating things we shouldn't be. The question before us all then is, are we willing to resist settling and risk pursuing excellence as our preferred way of being in the world? If so, then know this. The only way to break out of this rut is to commit to writing a new, more empowering *personal leadership story* of our own. One which affirms that the only way we can expect to spur transformation in our surroundings is to first do the work to begin a transformation in ourselves.

So get ready. What you'll find in this book will challenge you to burst that safe bubble you call your comfort zone. Intentionally pushing you beyond the narrow confines of the status quo so you can stretch and grow into the leader you want to be and those around you deserve to see. Not just for your benefit, mind you, but because if there was ever a time our nation needs its citizenry to discover the full transformative truth behind this centuries-old legend of the willing burden bearer, that time is now. After all, every legend exists because it possesses some degree of truth. My hope is that by the time you're done reading you too will be convinced this particular legend should be far less a myth and much more a rule about how each of us should strive to lead our own lives each and every day.

Enjoy the journey!

Don't Ignore Warnings

*When the country is in chaos, everybody has a plan to fix it—but
it takes a leader of real understanding to straighten things out.*
—Proverbs 28:2

WARNING
*This book will challenge the way you think about your
role in the world. Willingly applying what you find in
these pages will not only equip you to regularly reject
mediocrity, but it could very well persuade you to forever
change how you choose to define leadership.*

It may seem odd that I've started this book with a warning. But please
know I do so with a very deliberate purpose.

For over two decades I've been privileged to be a member of one of
the noblest professions anyone can be a part of—the US military. As an
officer and aviator serving in the United States Air Force, I have been
afforded the opportunity to defend the ideals of democracy across scores
of countries and promote the principles of peace on six continents. I've

also been extremely fortunate to lead some of the nation's finest men and women at home and abroad. Together, we've sought to do our small part in attracting people to a democratic way of life that values freedom and is committed to creating conditions for people to thrive, individually and collectively.

As a lifelong military aviator, I've also been able to fly a host of jet aircraft. However, regardless of how different the airframes may have been, one item has always been constant. We call it the Dash-1.

The Dash-1 is much like the owner's manual for your car, although significantly more complex and infinitely more voluminous. In addition to outlining common operating guidelines and procedures for properly employing the airplane, one section stands out more than the others: chapter three. This chapter provides details on irregular, abnormal, and emergency operations. In fact, the information in this chapter is deemed of such high importance that every page is outlined in a black-and-white checkered border that makes it easy to find and impossible to miss. Everyone who has ever flown a military aircraft, regardless of service, is intimately familiar with this chapter of their respective Dash-1s.

Given a pilot can face a wide range of possible challenging situations or malfunctions, wise people years ago developed a means to help further channel our attention. That is, they devised a way to categorize the information in this critical section of our flight manuals into three subareas, with each denoting increasing levels of potential consequences if some form of action is not eventually taken.

Notes, Cautions, and Warnings

The first category is termed a *note*. Notes provide information that is good to know but will likely not lead to any form of injury or catastrophe if you choose to ignore it. Thus, notes make us aware of useful and often ordinary things about operating our aircraft *smartly*.

In our daily lives, notes are akin to the stickers affixed to the inside of our windshields reminding us to change our oil at three-thousand miles. Although it's very unlikely anything disastrous will immediately happen if you don't pay attention, the sticker does serve as a visual reminder that you should consider doing something if you want to minimize the chances you'll do lasting damage to your car's engine in the future.

The second category is known as a *caution* and, as the term implies, is designed to heighten our awareness. A caution brings to light a situation that deserves increased vigilance, consideration, or coordination. These cautions then point us to important information about operating our aircraft *safely*.

For example, a caution in the Dash-1 is very much like hearing from your doctor that your cholesterol or blood pressure is elevated. If you fail to make some reasonable lifestyle changes in the not-too-distant future, your chance of experiencing more serious problems increases dramatically.

Taken together then, notes and cautions help us navigate life smartly and safely. They serve as convenient reminders of how paying attention to the small things in the present can help guard us from being overwhelmed by larger, more daunting circumstances in the future.

The final category is a *warning*, which alerts us to the fact we have a very real problem. We are taught from day one in pilot training to take warnings very, very seriously. Ignore a warning and you risk potentially devastating consequences to yourself, your aircraft, and very often those around you. In fact, many of the warnings present in our flight manuals are the result of people learning lessons the hard way—frequently taking the form of aircraft destroyed and lives lost.

Warnings, then, are designed to help us improve things in our surroundings by compelling us to take some form of corrective action, *immediately*.

In our personal lives, a warning is what we experience when we continue to ignore an event that threatens to drain the life out of us, be it a strained relationship, failing business, or dying dream. Anything that positions us to be paralyzed by hopelessness or potentially leaves us feeling powerless to influence outcomes if we fail to take some form of corrective action is a warning. But warnings are not limited to individuals. They, in fact, extend to entire societies.

Troubling Times

The warning signs that our society is experiencing a very real *personal leadership* crisis are everywhere. You only need to turn on the TV, tune into a radio program, click on the Internet, or pick up any periodical to find that story after story recounts a sad, sordid tale of broken promises, plundered pensions, and selfish motives by many of those entrusted to positions of authority and responsibility.[1] In once high-flying companies such as Enron, Arthur Anderson, WorldCom, and Tyco, it was the leaders' apathy, inaction, and lack of accountability that directly led to millions of innocent people being negatively affected, forever.

Of course, lapses in leadership are not limited to just the business world. For example, the inexcusable abuses at the Iraqi military prison in Abu Ghraib and the seemingly endless string of politicians facing ethical and moral charges continue to shake our confidence in leaders at every level. Perhaps it should be no surprise then that almost 80 percent of respondents in a recent Gallup poll think the moral values of our nation are getting worse instead of better.[2] And according to a recent survey by Harvard University, a majority of Americans confirm we suffer from a serious leadership crisis in America. Perhaps more importantly, even more believe the United States will decline as a nation without better leaders.[3]

Sadly, it seems as though mediocrity has become the new norm as it relates to how many of us think about leadership. Instead of the term leader being synonymous with someone who strives to use their influence to build value into their surroundings, it is more likely we associate it with someone doing whatever it takes just to keep the routine going. Whereas leadership was once a term that engendered inspiration, now it frequently invokes a sense of desperation as we collectively witness our nation's infrastructure crumble, medical costs skyrocket, deficits soar, school system's slip, marriages fizzle, and poverty, crime, hunger, homelessness, drug use, and a host of other challenges keep many citizen's struggling to survive and unable to thrive.

What all this confirms is that we don't just have a leadership crisis in America. Rather, in the words of Starbucks CEO Howard Schultz, what we are experiencing is nothing short of an all-out leadership *"emergency."*[4]

And we know it.

But thankfully, it doesn't have to stay this way. We can each choose, instead, to adopt a broader view of our potential role in the world—one that affirms the reality we cannot continue to expect to effectively tackle today's challenges by pursuing one-size-fits-all solutions or by relying on "expert" opinions. Effectively navigating ourselves beyond the present *mess we're in* can only begin if each of us *first* opens ourselves to thinking differently about what it really means to be a leader.

Rethinking Our View of Leadership

From our earliest memories it seems the guardians of the status quo, those who like things exactly as they exist in the present, work overtime to convince us leading is something reserved for a special few. It's something someone else does until we ourselves earn the appropriate promotion, attain the proper position, or win the next election. So what's the effect of our possessing such a limited perspective? Well, perhaps not surprisingly, it makes it altogether too convenient for each of us continue to abdicate responsibility for our role in permitting, promoting, and even protecting the existing state of affairs.

What if I told you this incomplete view of leadership is one of the primary reasons we in America continue to find ourselves facing such troubling times? Be it out of either ignorance or convenience, many of us have failed to realize the very concept of leadership was never intended to be interpreted in such confining ways. Begging the question "what was leadership originally meant to be?"

The word *leader* originates from the Indo-European root word *leit,* which was the name given to the person who carried the flag in front of an army advancing into battle. This person often had no positional authority and possessed no special title or rank.[5] Nonetheless, it was considered an honor and a privilege to carry a nation's colors into conflict on behalf of one's country or in support of one's cause or campaign.

The willingness of these courageous flag carriers to bear this burden of responsibility, however, posed some very real personal hazards. Most notably, it dramatically increased their chances of being injured or even killed in the process of carrying out their mission. This makes their commitment to going first, despite their knowing the potential cost to self, all the more noteworthy.

But beyond the nobility of their actions, it's important to understand there are several very deliberate reasons why the original definition of leadership was intentionally derived from this particular imagery. First, the flag bearer's selfless example reveals how setting off in new directions demands someone first *know the way.*[6] Serving as a reminder that one

> **NOTE**
> *One of the primary roles of a leader is to help guide others toward a future they can influence, liberating them from a past they cannot change*

of the primary roles of a leader is to help guide others toward a future they can influence, liberating them from a past they cannot change.

Second, this image provides a compelling picture of how leading also entails someone possessing the willingness to *show others the way*. What good is it for someone to cast a vision or propose a plan if they aren't willing to point people in the direction they should go to achieve it? And finally, while *knowing the way* and *showing the way* are noble in their own right, leadership ultimately demands that the one bearing responsibility for carrying the flag be the first to *go the way* before they can expect others to consider following suit.[7] After all, leading denotes action; action demands movement; and movement is how the process of positive progress we routinely refer to as change gets set into motion. Testimony to how all talk and no walk doesn't make a leader. It's *our example* that persuades those around us to abandon the safety of the status quo in pursuit of new territory.

So, with this in mind, how might things improve in our homes, workplaces, worship spaces, and communities if at all levels of society we began to view leading less as a noun and more as a verb? Instead of thinking about leadership in terms of a static title, rank, position, or role we possess, what if we chose to see leading as something we do every time we choose to walk differently in the world by *accepting responsibility for taking the initiative to promote the positive change we want to see occur in our surroundings*? No matter where we currently find ourselves in the proverbial hierarchy, organizational chart, or established social order.

Time Is of the Essence

In 2011, our nation was shocked when prominent Pennsylvania State University leaders, including the late legendary football coach Joe Paterno, were accused of ignoring allegations of child sex abuse by the school's former defensive coordinator almost a decade earlier. In addition to tarnishing a university's once-sterling reputation, shattering the trust of an entire sport, and prematurely ending the career of a coach with the most victories in collegiate history, it leaves all of us wondering, "How can something like this happen?"

The sad truth is that their failure didn't happen overnight. It was the result of warnings ignored, in the form of abdicated responsibility, missed opportunity, and a lack of commitment to stand up for the very values these leaders espoused, publicly and privately. Not only will the price of their silence be measured in terms of tens of millions of dollars, but also in reputations lost and lives forever ruined. Made all the worse, I might add, by the fact that many of the victims were participants in the not-for-profit foundation the abuser created to help at-risk youth get a new start on life.

This latest very public leadership failure speaks clearly to the reason why this book needs to be written, and written now. Every one of us must choose to recognize that warnings are more blessings than they are bad things. They're a call to action to step up to life's challenges instead of back down from them; an opportunity to abandon what's not working in order to build toward something that will.

History and experience continues to affirm that the true leaders in our society are

> **NOTE**
>
> *The true leaders in our society are those whose performance and attitude exceed our expectations when the chips are down and hard things need to get done*

those whose performance and attitude exceed our expectations when the chips are down and hard things need to get done. They are the people in our midst who are the sparks of progress in our homes, workplaces, worship spaces and communities whose titles may not accurately reflect their status—the men and women unafraid to say no to the status quo and yes to doing something to create conditions for nobler values to take root and blossom in their surroundings—one opportunity at a time.

Parting Thoughts

Poet Walt Kelly coined a phrase for a 1970 earth day poster that eloquently and appropriately captures the essence of the challenges facing our society. "We have met the enemy…and he is us." In other words, when it comes to promoting positive change in our surroundings, we are either part of the problem or part of the solution.

There can be no more fence-sitting.

Rather than accepting that we each possess a whole host of unique talents, gifts, skills, and strengths that can help transform conditions in our part of the world, too many of us today seem strangely content to accept mediocrity as the norm. Instead of seeing the status quo as more reference point than boundary marker, we all too frequently allow ourselves to settle for taking the path of least resistance—abdicating personal responsibility for using the full measure of our influence to do something to try and move things forward around us.

Family Life President and CEO Dennis Rainey writes in his book *Stepping Up* that "doing nothing is like gravity; it just happens. Nothing is the fruit of passivity. Nothing is the consequence of a lack of conviction… Doing nothing expresses no risk, exerts no initiative, and experiences no reward or triumph…the easiest thing to do is nothing."[8]

In a fast paced world that is more volatile, uncertain, complex, and ambiguous than perhaps at any other time in recorded human history, doing nothing is not an option. Why? Because burying our heads in the sand and going with the flow, blindly accepting others people's ideas and opinions about how we should lead our lives while remaining oblivious to our own biases and blind spots just doesn't work.

In fact, it never really has.

Author Thomas Barnett once wisely shared how life consistently improves for humanity overtime. It does so, however, only when people take it upon themselves not only to imagine a future worth creating, but actually get busy trying to build it themselves. His words serving to remind us how striving to lead our lives in a more excellent way begins by recognizing that warnings are *the fuel of change:* wake up calls designed to remind us we have a very real problem on our hands that demands we take some form of corrective action, now!

So please consider this book a Dash-1 of sorts. A practical guide to help each of us better understand how leading ourselves beyond the mess we're in is foremost *an inside job*. One that begins by determining which warnings we may be currently missing or ignoring in our own homes, workplaces, worship spaces, or communities and then committing to doing something about them.

Why continue to wait and risk learning our lessons the hard way?

Part One

REDEFINING OUR
BOUNDARY MARKERS

We are all born originals—
why is it so many of us die copies?
—Edward Young

Chapter 1

The Mess We're In

Conformity is the jailer of freedom and the enemy of growth.
—John F. Kennedy

It is no secret that America was founded primarily as a land of opportunity. A "field of dreams" built on an ethic of personal responsibility and an abiding faith in positive progress.[9]

Almost entirely a nation of immigrants, ours is a country of promise in which people of all races, religions, or nationalities can experience everything from new beginnings to happy endings to even their wildest dreams and aspirations. As the first-generation son of immigrants myself, I continue to firmly believe the diversity wrought from this "melting pot" of people remains one of our nation's greatest strengths.

But this does not mean we are a nation devoid of difficult experiences. The host of dynamic challenges and daunting problems we face are certainly not the first (or the worst) we've encountered as a country. In fact, our history is replete with ups and downs. We've experienced moments of elation, such as our victories in the Revolutionary War and two World Wars, as well as our development of a national space program that successfully landed the first man on the moon.

Of course, we know heartbreak, too. Our own Civil War and, less than a century later the unpopular conflict in Vietnam, left us broken and bitterly divided for a season. However, nothing has shaken the country's confidence in itself and its future more than the Great Depression. Almost overnight, the world's most prosperous nation found itself with scores of people dazed, confused, and outright filled with fear. With millions suddenly out of work, more businesses failing daily, and people's confidence plummeting quickly, for the first time in our history "the American Dream" seemed doomed.

Much like today, our nation was on the ropes.

Well-intentioned government leaders stepped in to fill the ever-growing void between hope and fear, creating a slew of new programs to help get the country back on its feet. Welfare, a by-product of the Social Security Act of 1932, was born as a safety net for the nation's most vulnerable citizens. It was a bold move designed to address a very real challenge to our collective existence. But this attempt to do good on a massive scale produced an unanticipated casualty: *the ethic of personal responsibility.* And just like that, the slippery slope of accepting mediocrity as the norm, usually without a fight, had insidiously begun.

A Collapsing Ethic—Responsibility

Interestingly, it was not the unprecedented government bailout programs of the era that ended the Great Depression—it was World War II. With the very real threat of our cherished way of life at stake, we once again returned to old form. Selfishness was out and selflessness back in, as people across our society rolled up their sleeves to do anything they could for the cause at hand.

Whether it was buying war bonds, riveting aircraft wings and fuselages in factories, or donning the cloth of the nation to take the fight to the enemy, America's citizens were once again "all in." Men, women, and even children did what they had to do to both plant and water the seeds of victory. And because of people's willingness at all levels of society to do what they could, when they could, where they could to be part of the solution to the challenge at hand, victory was ours. The ability to set aside personal agendas and accept responsibility for doing something to support the collective good set our nation on a path to once again flourish and thrive.

The years following World War II were nothing short of spectacular for America on many fronts. Confidence swelled, optimism soared, and the economy boomed. The future looked brighter than ever as productivity skyrocketed and our standard of living followed suit. Houses got bigger, cars flashier, and money looser. Success was everywhere. And, as is often the case when good times roll, many people began taking things for granted.

For the next several decades, both government and business, flush with profits and awash in ideas on how to build an ever-more-prosperous society, began an unprecedented spending spree. Government steadily swelled in size as it pursued ambitious agendas, and corporate America followed suit. Although not evil by design or intention, this extended period of overpromise and inflating expectations led our nation and many of its citizens to become overconfident and, to be blunt, outright unrealistic in their desires and demands. Our growing individual and collective appetites for "more and more" blinded us to the fact that we were programming ourselves, personally, professionally, and nationally, into an unsustainable situation.

Quite unintentionally, *we fell prey to the lie that success was a right we deserved rather than a privilege we must continue to earn.* And just like that, the ethic of personal and collective responsibility, our nation's true source of strength, began to collapse. Selfishness, propelled

> **CAUTION**
>
> *Quite unintentionally, we fell prey to the lie that success was a right we deserved rather than a privilege we must continue to earn*

by slick marketing campaigns and the nonstop introduction of neat new products designed to make us look younger, feel thinner, or appear happier once again displaced selflessness. A growing sense of individual entitlement overshadowed the importance of maintaining accountability for one's personal state of affairs.

What few realized, until recently, was that this ever-growing sense of entitlement was predicated on a fatally flawed assumption: that our nation could maintain its position of unchecked power, explosive productivity, and unparalleled profitability forever. Despite finding ourselves in a rapidly changing world, we became so enamored with the status quo that we lost touch with reality. A reality that has since rudely descended upon us in the form of soaring deficits, a stagnated economy, sky-high unemployment, and a disillusioned and disheartened nation of citizens unsure how to break out of the current mess we're in.10

But here's some good news. The way out of this mess isn't as elusive as it may appear. In fact, if there is one thing history teaches us it's that when the challenges before us are most significant, we are often at our individual and collective best. Proof positive how the solution to every problem or challenge set before us is already present, invisible in plain sight, in the *example* of those leaders unafraid to go first in leading the change they want to see—those courageous men and women in our midst whose attitudes and actions clearly communicate "look, no more mediocre me."

Tough Start...Big Finish

Timothy was born into a family of ten children at the beginning of the Great Depression. His mother had been married three times and both parents were alcoholics. Their family occupied a series of apartments in the poorest neighborhoods of Newark, New Jersey. From nearby vacant lots, Timothy and his siblings frequently collected milkweed stems that their mother boiled into a broth for their dinner.

It was often their only meal of the day.

In the midst of their extreme poverty, Timothy was frequently abused and constantly reminded he would never amount to anything. Although he attended school, he was not considered a good student by any means. When he was 15, Timothy left home and never returned.

Shortly thereafter he made contact with a charity organization that connected him to a kindly man whose personal interest in Timothy made him feel valued and appreciated for the first time in his life. Timothy eventually graduated from high school in a distant city. No one from his family ever came looking for him in those early years. In fact, the only time they did seek him out was much, much later. Not to invite him home, but to ask for money.

Though underage, he enlisted in the Navy, where he was guaranteed a place to sleep, consistent rules and expectations, and three square meals a day. While on leave Timothy met his future wife and eloped, beginning a 52-year marriage.

The Navy remained Timothy's permanent address for years. His nearly 30 years of work there remains classified to this day, locked behind the doors of a high-level security clearance. During this time, Timothy, his wife, and their four children all graduated from college. Two of his children went on to earn master's degrees.

While in his fifties, Timothy was diagnosed with incurable cancer and underwent an extreme operation and experimental treatments in hopes of prolonging his life two years. He lived 19 more, despite each follow-up test confirming the existence of the ever-spreading deadly disease.

Timothy died a few days before his 77th birthday, having repeatedly beaten the odds that he would lead a mediocre existence. He passed away quietly with scores of family and friends close by, in his multimillion-dollar home paid in full. Throughout his life, he had the great joy of seeing his eight grandchildren join the family and to witness the eldest graduate from high school. For more than 15 years, he also served as a Sunday School superintendent and youth group leader, mentoring teens aspiring to become future military officers.

Hundreds of mourners attended his funeral. Many of them had been children and young adults he mentored. Everyone lovingly recalled Timothy's quiet strength, deep faith, and ever-present resolve to accept responsibility for improving conditions in his surroundings. He kept the secret of his childhood from nearly all of them, and they would never have guessed the problems and challenges he'd encountered in his early, youthful years.[11]

Although Timothy was not his real name, this is the true story of a leader who didn't allow his apparent limitations to dictate his future potential. One common person whose uncommon commitment to saying no to the status quo and yes to leading his life in a more excellent way reminds us we each already possess all the innate power and authority needed to accept responsibility for taking the initiative to promote the positive change we want to see occur in our surroundings.

We just have to choose to get in the game.

Why the Status Quo Must Go

Oscar winning actress Olympia Dukakis once remarked during an interview how, "most of us are not real eager to grow, myself included. We try to be happy by staying in the status quo. But if we're not willing to be honest with ourselves about what we feel, *we don't evolve.*"

I'm not sure when she spoke these words she knew just how correct she really was.

Evolutionary biologists, when speaking of the status quo, routinely use the term *prolonged equilibrium.* What they are describing is the scientific observation that when any living system enters a state of lethargy or complacency for too long, it becomes not only less responsive to changes occurring around it, but ultimately grows resistant to change altogether. Testimony to the fact that anytime we become too comfortable with the current state of affairs, be it in our personal or professional lives, our organizations, political structures, or anywhere else in our society for that matter, it becomes extremely difficult if not altogether impossible to flourish and thrive. Growth stops, atrophy sets in, and before we know it, we find ourselves with a mess.

A mess we could have prevented.

Today we find ourselves in such a mess. Everywhere we look, the status quo is hard at work convincing us it's better to stay put and keep doing more of the same. Be it bipartisan politics, narrow philosophical ideologies, or laws and policies promoting individual entitlement over personal responsibility, the status quo strives to keep us narrowly and selfishly focused. Divided instead of united, it compels us to work on individual agendas instead of toward collective solutions to persistent personal, professional, or societal problems.

In our own lives, the status quo refers to anything that is a barrier to forward motion—those individual, organizational, and relational obstacles that keep us from becoming the best version of ourselves. Be it a destructive habit, a persistent problem, or an undeveloped gift, the status quo strives to keep us squarely in our comfort zones and subtly persuades us *to accept mediocrity as the norm.* Helping us better understand why the late President Ronald Reagan was quite fond of reminding people that the status quo all too conveniently translates into the phrase, "the mess we're in."[12]

When Mediocrity Reigns

The dictionary aptly defines mediocrity as *"moderate to inferior in quality."* Derived from the French term of the same spelling, mediocre literally means "halfway up the mountain." Insinuating how accepting mediocrity is to fail to achieve one's objective or fall short of attaining one's potential. If I had only word to capture the essence of this definition I'd offer the term, *settling.*

Everywhere we look today it is apparent scores of us are content settling. By settling I mean despite our knowing there is a different way or a different plan that could help us move in the direction of our dreams, aspirations, and objectives, we choose instead to disengage and do or say nothing. And why shouldn't we? After all, going along with the herd instead of doing something to break from established convention is certainly safe. It keeps us from risking our well thought out career paths, prevents us from disrupting our finely honed promotion plans, or protects us from venturing too far outside our tightly scripted personal lines of responsibility so we can keep our circumstances secure, predictable, and above all, controllable. But any way you try to rationalize it, choosing to consistently settle for less than we are capable of doing and being hurts far more than it ever helps.

Now please don't get me wrong. We have all undoubtedly found ourselves in that awkwardly uncomfortable position of settling at one time or another on this journey we call life. But the real problem occurs when settling becomes the norm. Like a good habit gone bad; an addiction gone wild, the price of settling for mediocrity and refusing to bring our best selves to whatever it is we are doing costs all of us dearly.

WARNING

The status quo strives to keep us squarely in our comfort zones and persuades us to accept mediocrity as the norm

Need proof?

Economists estimate that an estimated $300 billion is lost every year due to disengaged employees. Gallup, one of the world's leading researchers in the area of personal and professional engagement and satisfaction levels, actually calculates the cost of mediocrity to the American economy to be as much as $350 billion per year in lost productivity.

Ouch.

Elaborating on these figures, Gallup researchers go on to describe how their findings reveal only 29% of American's in the workplace today are fully engaged in what they do. Even more startling is the fact these same statistics highlight how 58% of people are content sitting on the sidelines and accepting mediocrity as the norm.[13] Seemingly more interested in being spectators than they are being active contributors to the mission, task, or purpose at hand.

Of course, a mediocre me mindset doesn't just impact us at our work. It subtly infiltrates every facet of our lives, lowering our confidence, reducing our willpower, and zapping our motivation. All of which make us prone to do what is safe rather than what is right; doing what is desired instead of what is required; or worrying more about what people may say about us than about doing what is most important to us.

Here's the bottom line: Allowing mediocrity to influence all facets of our lives is insidious and dangerous. In addition to clouding our thinking and hindering our actions, it cultivates doubt for the future, stifles forward motion, and rationalizes away opportunities to innovate, stretch and grow. In simplest terms, mediocrity *paralyzes us in place*. It convinces us to ignore the warnings in our lives so the status quo can have its way with us—leading us to abdicate responsibility for taking the initiative to promote the positive change we want to see occur in our surroundings.

Parting Thoughts

It has been called the greatest photograph of all time. It may well be the most widely reproduced, even winning the Pulitzer Prize for photography. Snapped on February 23, 1945 as our nation was fighting its way across the Pacific as part of the island hopping campaign in World War II, it served as the symbol for the Seventh War Loan Drive; was used on a postage stamp; appeared on the cover of countless magazines and newspapers across the globe; and even served as the model for the Marine Corps War Memorial that today stands in Arlington, Virginia. A timeless symbol of the cost we must be willing to bear in defending the values, ideas, and principles this great nation was originally founded upon.

The famous picture of five marines and a navy corpsman struggling to raise the flag atop Mount Suribachi on the tiny island of Iwo Jima in the middle of the Pacific Ocean perfectly captures the sense of momentum of six men straining toward a common goal. In this instance, that goal was to mark claim to the most strategic point on the island following one of the costliest battles in Marine Corps history. Its toll of 6,821 Americans dead, 5,931 of them Marines, accounted for nearly one-third of all Marine Corps losses in all of World War II.

Eyewitness accounts confirm that the raising of the flag on the fourth day of the bloody battle of Iwo Jima ignited a wave of energy and enthusiasm that could be heard across the island. Just as the battle was bogging down and progress was reduced to mere inches an hour, the moment that red, white, and blue of our nation's flag was seen proudly flying atop that hilltop, American troops were all filled with a new found vigor and vitality. The momentum of that moment subsequently inspired them to push through to achieve the mission of conquering what would become the first Japanese homeland soil to be captured by the Americans.

Much like the courageous flag carriers of old who willingly raised their hand to bear the burden of knowing, showing, and going the way, these six men remind us of the true definition of leadership. That is, it's not designed to be a position we earn or seek but rather is meant to be a responsibility we choose to fulfill. A choice to step outside our comfort zones and do what we can, when we can, where we can to have more impact, make more of a difference, and lead lives of true purpose, meaning, and significance.

On my desk at home sits a copy of the 1950 edition of *The Armed Forces Officer*, a small booklet outlining the roles, responsibilities, and expectations of military leaders. I believe the first paragraph gets to the heart of what it means to lead well, in or out of uniform. It reads: "Having been specifically chosen by the United States to sustain the dignity and integrity of its sovereign power, an officer [leader] is expected to maintain himself, and so exert his influence for so long as he may live, that he will be recognized as a worthy symbol of *all that is best in the national character.*"[14]

Although the booklet doesn't explain in detail what the phrase "best in the national character" specifically entails, I believe it serves to remind us that we are at our best as a people and as a country not when we are standing still, paralyzed in place in a state of *prolonged equilibrium,* but rather when we *choose* to do something to reject mediocrity and keep things solidly moving forward in our individual and collective spheres of influence.

WARNING
Mediocrity is insidious and dangerous…it clouds our thinking and hinders our actions, cultivating doubt of the future

Remember, be it in science, medicine, the military, politics, religion, academics, or any other walk of life for that matter, it is those who risk thinking differently than the masses, exercise the courage to act differently than the masses, and possess the strength of character to be different than the masses who make the greatest mark on our world. They are the catalysts of positive change in our society who understand that when good leadership is plentiful, it's an afterthought. But when good leadership is absent, it should become our only thought.

Chapter 2

Sparks of Positive Change

Each person must live their life as a model for others.
—Rosa Parks

By all counts, Dr. Gary Parker had it made. A West Los Angeles specialist in oral and maxillofacial surgery, his specialized training and blossoming private practice all but guaranteed he could lead a life filled with material comforts. However, Dr. Parker, insistent on using his talents not to cater to Hollywood's elite but to serve the greater good, chose a different route. Seeing medicine as a means to address deeper social, spiritual, and economic human needs, Dr. Parker walked away from society's interpretation of success—and happiness—and joined the global charity, Mercy Ships, in 1987.

And he has never looked back.

"Some thought I was quite mad," the doctor acknowledges with a grin about his counterintuitive decision.[15] Leaving behind a comfortable Western lifestyle to live and work for almost two decades on a 522-foot ship named the *Anastasis*, which for over a quarter of a century has been delivering hope and healing off the coast of Africa, just isn't what people expect a plastic surgeon to do.[16] Nevertheless, Dr. Parker, now the ship's chief medical officer, would have it no other way. Joined by his wife Susan, an educator he met and married aboard the ship, he can think of nothing more rewarding than doing his part in treating the facial tumors and deformities that can be found upon thousands of the forgotten poor.[17]

Dr. Parker, a humble man of faith, is quick to point out he has no regrets about giving up some measure of personal comfort in order to do his part to serve humanity. His willingness to stand out from the crowd reflects his strong belief that we all have a responsibility to use our God-given gifts to benefit others. His only disappointment being that he cannot help every patient. Not every tumor is operable or benign, and a cleft lip and palate is not always the patient's only problem. Nonetheless, this doesn't deter him from doing all he can to improve the quality of life for those he encounters.[18]

Committed to being a force for good in the lives of some of the most marginalized people in the world—the diseased, deformed, and scarred individuals often outcast from African village societies—Dr. Parker remains convinced, in his own words, that "for hope to be credible in the future, it needs to be tangible in the present." This doesn't happen "by accident," he adds.[19] Someone has to assume the responsibility to educate, enlighten, inspire, care, love, and lead others to a better, brighter future. Moreover, because of leaders like Dr. Parker and hundreds of selfless volunteers at Mercy Ships, many of those in Africa who can barely breathe or eat, or who may be dying from suffocation and malnutrition as their deformities block their airways, now have a new opportunity at life.[20]

Emma Goldman once remarked how it is "The idealists and visionaries foolish enough to throw caution to the winds and express their ardor and faith in some supreme deed" who have advanced and enriched our world the most. The truth of the matter is, every time we push the boundaries of our comfort zones in an effort to improve things in our part of the world, we guard ourselves from becoming an unwitting captive to a mediocre me mindset. Opening ourselves in the process to leading a life of true relevance, significance, and dare I say…excellence.

Mediocrity's Silent Accomplice

Stories like Dr. Parker's encourage and inspire us by reflecting humanity operating at its best. His willingness to reject mediocrity and accept responsibility for proactively doing something to improve conditions in his sphere of influence provides us a compelling illustration of leadership in its most basic, fundamental form. However, as inspiring as his example may be, we are likely left wondering why it's so challenging for most of us to break free from our well entrenched habit patterns and abandon our regular routines to pursue our passions, goals, aspirations, and dreams. What is it about mediocrity that leads us to so easily settle for average when we know we are capable of so much more? Let me share a story with you that will help illuminate the powerful, invisible force at work in all our lives that strives to convince us to make playing it safe our default option.

At 8:17 pm on March 3, 1943, an air raid alarm erupted in the skies over London, England. People heard the sounds and almost instantaneously began to experience panic. Bus drivers immediately stopped their buses. Motorists horridly pulled their cars to the side of the road. Pedestrians began searching for the nearest shelter to shield them from the attack they were certain would come.

Anti-aircraft artillery could be heard in the nearby distance and citizens continued to look skyward for the now familiar silhouette of the Nazi warplanes. Although not a single plane could be seen, the level of hysteria amongst the crowd began to escalate.

Intent on finding shelter, scores of British citizens raced in the direction of an underground subway station called Bethnal Green. As the terrified citizens descended the stairs into the interior of the protective station, a young mother carrying her baby lost her footing and fell. Her unexpected tumble immediately threw off the rhythm of the hurried crowd behind her and in a matter of seconds, people began to fall one on top of the other. At the same time, another wave of safety seekers, afraid the station would fill before they could seek protective cover, began pressing ever more firmly on those people ahead of them at the top of the stairs. What ensued was fifteen minutes of deadly chaos.

It took four hours for rescue workers to disentangle the bodies in Bethnal Green station. In the end, 173 people, including 62 children, perished that evening and not a single enemy bomb had been dropped. It wasn't a German bomber raid that claimed all those innocent victims. It was something far more insidious: *fear.*[21]

Fear, Fear Everywhere

As a friend of mine once shared, "fear loves a good stampede," and as this unfortunate true story affirms, fear's payday is frequently heightened panic, shaken confidence, and frantic decision-making.[22] If we take notice of what is happening in our world right now, fear is making a very good living lately. Just click on the news, switch on the radio, or connect to the internet and we will certainly encounter story after story that may well leave us scurrying for cover ourselves.

Pause and think about it. The ever present threat of global warming; the discovery of pesticides in our food or the identification of a new form of cancer; daily reminders of an almost certain pending global financial calamity; the unexpected massacre of innocent children in a school, people in a movie theater, house of worship, and college campus, and the list goes on and on. In fact, fear has become such a pervasive topic in our world that one psychologist has cited that children today are living with the same amount of fear in their daily lives as a psychiatric patient did in the 1950's.

Dr. Jack Haskings, a professor at the University of Tennessee, has spent well over a decade studying the detrimental effects of media on people. His findings, in addition to confirming the powerful effect regular exposure to negative news has on building fear and anxiety into our lives, also provide us a powerful reminder as to why mediocrity so frequently and so easily becomes our preferred response.

In one particularly noteworthy research project, Dr. Haskings set out to determine the influence a five-minute radio program would have on how people perceive and internalize what they hear or see occurring around them. Haskins exposed one group of people to several weeks of news that was filled with nothing but negativity: an earthquake that kills thousands, a terrorist attack on a school bus, a random shooting in a supermarket, riots in the streets of a large city, and so on. At the same time, he established a control group that was subject to only positive, uplifting news.

At the end of the project, Haskins discovered four very discernible effects on those people consistently exposed to the five-minute daily barrage of negative information:

- They were more depressed than before;
- They believed the world was a negative place;
- They were less likely to help others;
- They began to believe that what they heard would soon happen to them.[23]

In a nutshell, Dr. Haskins confirmed how consistently being exposed to fearful, negative events has a very profound effect on how we choose to lead our lives. This study also reinforces what psychologists and sociologists have been telling us for years. Namely, the thoughts we entertain in our minds quickly become the thoughts that guide our lives. So much so, in fact, that it seems reasonable to assert that if being exposed to only five minutes of negative news can leave us feeling this discouraged, disappointed, and disempowered, it should be no surprise fear has such an easy time convincing us to narrow our field of vision and adopt a greatly diminished view of our potential role on the world—helping us understand that we are today where our thoughts have brought us and we will be tomorrow where our thoughts will take us—for better or worse.

Fear: A Persistent Obstacle to Positive Progress

If we are honest with ourselves, we'll discover fear plagues many of us. It is an unfriendly companion that blocks creativity, kills curiosity, and paralyzes us in place. At a personal level, fear undermines our relationships and hinders us from growing into the best version of ourselves. Professionally, fear creates a barrier to accomplishment that limits success, narrows focus and diminishes morale. Communally, fear causes us to build higher walls around our neighborhoods, put bigger bars on our windows, or stronger locks on our front doors. In simplest terms, fear becomes a filter that convinces us to accept mediocrity as the norm in how we choose to lead our lives each and every day.

Admittedly, fear, commonly defined as a physical and emotional response to a perceived threat or danger, is not inherently bad. In fact, researchers who specialize in studying the brain confirm that since our arrival on the planet, fear has been an essential tool to protect and preserve human life.[24] Serving as the proverbial canary in the coalmine, fear is an internal alarm system designed to *warn us* to pay attention to what is occurring around us so we can take some form of corrective action before it is too late.

From such a perspective, perhaps it's should not be a surprise that cognitive scientists have discovered our brains, in an effort to effectively deal with the warnings occurring around us, are actually hard-wired to *fear first* and *think second*. This helps to explain why by the time we begin to experience fear *physiologically*, be it sweaty palms, trembling hands, or a racing heart, our bodies are already hard at work trying to keep us safe by automatically setting into motion our flight or fight response. Proving firsthand how fear can indeed be a friend and not merely a foe.

The challenge arises, however, when fear is allowed to continue to operate unchecked. Much like the panicked citizens in London in 1943 who unsuspectingly raced headlong to their deaths in that subway corridor, fear likes to send us ducking for cover at the first sign of danger or discomfort. It tricks us into believing we have lost control of our circumstances and if there is one thing that bothers human beings more than anything else does, it is feeling as though we have lost control of what is happening in our lives.

WARNING

Fear…serves as the proverbial canary in the coalmine that alerts us to potential danger

This subtle but significant phenomenon helps explain why so many of us do not like disrupting our routines and trying new things. I am not just talking about willfully attempting particularly unnerving endeavors such as skydiving, mountain climbing, or bungee jumping. I am referring to attempting anything *different* that can leave us feeling less in control of circumstances than we prefer. Helping us to understand why it is so easy for the status quo to persuade us to accept mediocrity as the norm and abandon our quest to try and lead our lives in a more excellent way.

Overcoming Fear in Our Lives

As we've discovered, fear can be a particularly powerful force in our lives that creates the illusion it is helping us restore control over what is amiss in our surroundings. In truth, however, fear leads us to limit our personal lines of responsibility and causes us to settle for the perceived safety of sticking with the status quo. Subtly setting us on a path to adopt a flawed way of thinking and being in the world that erroneously convinces us that pursuing mediocrity is the most appropriate way to navigate the present mess we are in.

How do we conquer fear so we can begin leading our lives in a more excellent way? Well that is actually a trick question. In truth, those who consistently make the greatest positive impact in their spheres of influence understand we don't actually have to "conquer" fear. We simply have to take proactive steps to do something to try and *master* it.

Mark Twain once said, "courage is resistance to fear, mastery of fear—not absence of fear." The key to saying no to the status quo and yes to leading our lives in a more excellent way does not demand we defeat fear. We just have to be willing to face our fears head on. For example, one of the most pervasive fears people across society possess is public speaking. Too many, just the mere thought of standing in front of a crowd makes them break out in a cold sweat, sending waves of anxiety throughout their system. I, on the other hand, love speaking to groups. Nevertheless, like most people, I still get nervous before I set foot on stage. My palms sweat, my mind races, and I can't help but think about my greatest fear, "what if I bomb?" But when the moment comes to take the platform, I choose to set that fear aside and *lean into the opportunity set before me.* In other words, I master my fear not by allowing it to convince me to accept mediocrity and skip speaking all together, but rather by committing to giving my best possible performance in that moment. Trusting that regardless how it turns out, I can find confidence in knowing I'm getting just a little better today than I was yesterday by choosing

> **NOTE**
> *We can accomplish just about anything in life if we are willing to reject mediocrity and face our fears head-on*

to do something to willingly push the bounds of my abilities and stretch the full extent of my capabilities.

The lesson for all of us in this illustration is that the more we choose to lean into our fears, the more confidence we build in ourselves. The more confidence we build in ourselves, the more in control we feel over our circumstances. And the more in control we feel, the more likely we are to accept responsibility for taking the initiative to act on opportunities to try and have more of an impact and make more of a difference—setting us on a path to lead a life of true purpose, meaning, and significance in the process.

Parting Thoughts

It's important to note that breaking free from the grip of mediocrity in order to get busy building the future we imagine doesn't demand we proceed fearlessly or recklessly. After all, the real heroes of society, those who freely give the best of themselves to serve a purpose greater than themselves, teach us that fear is an emotion that can either send us scurrying for safety underground or propel us forward to seek higher ground. It either leads us to settle for a life that is "good enough," or motivates us to try new things so we can move ever closer to becoming the best version of ourselves possible—one opportunity at a time.

The great American philosopher and writer Henry David Thoreau once went to jail rather than pay a tax to a state that supported slavery. While in jail, he used the time to write his most important literary work. His essay "Civil Disobedience" has helped people from all walks of life discover that anyone who strives to make their mark on the world must be willing to march to the beat of a different drummer without being afraid of being out of step with the crowd.

Thoreau's close friend, Ralph Waldo Emerson, another great American philosopher and writer, came to visit him in jail and upon arrival asked him: "Why Henry, what are you doing in there?" To which Thoreau quickly responded, "Nay Ralph, the question is, what are you doing out there?"

More than ever, in a culture that has come to expect leaders to fight for their rights, push their way to the top, and always look out for number one, we find ourselves starved for a different model of leadership. In other words, we are hungry for examples of people like Timothy and Dr. Parker who are willing to go against the grain and help build value into their surroundings—men and women less interested in casting stones or pointing fingers of blame at others when something isn't working but instead, who are ready to get busy helping solve the challenges set before us.

But don't just take my word for it.

A recent survey by a prominent national magazine reveals that seventy-six percent of respondents think the country is on the wrong track. Seventy percent believe the country was better at solving its problems 25 years ago than it is today. Sadly, statistic after statistic reveals that America is underperforming in virtually every sector of our society. Not because we're aren't smart enough, creative enough, or capable enough. The reason is much simpler and straightforward. We've surrendered our ethic of personal responsibility to the status quo, which just won't easily let go.

Perhaps this is why the same study that reveals the bulk of Americans believe our country is heading in the wrong direction also illuminates a more important truth. Namely, it confirms that the vast majority of our nation's citizens are not interested in looking to institutions or politicians to solve our society's problems. Instead of placing our confidence in the hands of those who have been formally elected, appointed, or anointed to positions of power and influence we prefer to put our trust in *one another* to help improve our circumstances.

No special position, title, rank, or role required.

It is interesting to note that Thoreau didn't seem to have much to show for his years on earth when he died of tuberculosis in his mid-forties. But his commitment to making a stand against the status quo, as articulated in his essay on civil disobedience, has gone on to make a profound impact on history. In fact, fifty years after Thoreau penned the now famous words of his essay, Gandhi cited it as his source of inspiration for leading India's people to independence from British rule and a century after Thoreau's death, Martin Luther King, Jr., based his efforts to advance civil rights on the words of Thoreau and the courageous example of Gandhi.[25] Proving yet again how seizing the initiative and accepting responsibility to make some form of contribution, even a seemingly small contribution, can make a world of positive difference...even if we don't experience the results of our actions right away.

Remember, defeating mediocrity is about overcoming our fears so we can get busy creating the life we've always wanted. This, of course, will not happen by accident—it must be intentional—a byproduct of our willingness to walk differently in the world for the purpose of setting an example worth emulating.

Leaving each of us to answer the question for ourselves: "*What are we doing out there*" to leave the world a little better tomorrow than we found it today?

Chapter 3

Invisible in Plain Sight

Do not go where the path may lead. Go, instead,
where there is no path and leave a trail.
—Ralph Waldo Emerson

The ancient mystic Nasrudin, a hallmark of Middle Eastern folklore, was allegedly fond of telling this particular story.

There was once a wealthy, notorious smuggler who, posing as simple merchant, was constantly crossing the desert frontier with his string of donkeys, his saddle bags loaded with nothing more than water and straw. The custom directors in the region were certain he was carrying some form of contraband that would account for his great wealth. Year after year they stopped him, yet the search of the saddlebags always yielded the same result: nothing more than water and straw. One day while relaxing at a local teahouse, the now-retired smuggler encountered the former chief of customs. The retired official could not help but ask the inevitable question: "Now that we are old men who have entered retirement and are no longer a threat to one another, please tell me, during all those years, what were you smuggling?"

The wealthy smuggler, with a kind smile, simply replied: "Donkeys." [26]

Invisible in Plain Sight

I've always loved this story because it serves as a simple, yet profound reminder how often the most valuable things in our lives are right in front of us—*invisible in plain sight.*

CAUTION
When something becomes commonplace, we have a tendency to neglect it or just plain look past it

Think about the simple truth of these words: invisible in plain sight. What this speaks to is the natural human tendency to take certain things for granted. For instance, we don't really notice each time we take a breath, do we? We don't notice the pavement we walk on, unless we trip because we didn't see the twist or buckle in the pavement, right? Nor do we tend to question whether the sun will come up, or the chair will support our weight when we sit down, or that our bodies will move when we will them to.

Closer to home, we each may have fallen into the trap at one time or another of taking the person we love for granted. Or maybe it's our good health, a close friend, our job, or even a gift or talent we unintentionally ignore. The fact of the matter is, when something becomes commonplace, we have a tendency to neglect it or just plain look past it. It's so obvious it's almost as if we develop a blind spot of sorts to the value, beauty, or wisdom present right in front of us.

Being a student of change leadership most of my adult life, you can only imagine how surprised I was to discover that I, like millions of others, have been unintentionally looking past the deeper meaning hidden within the legend of the willing burden bearer all these years. [27] It was an unexpected discovery that helped me recognize how we each already possess everything required to regularly reject mediocrity and intentionally embrace excellence in every facet of our lives.

Let me tell you what I found.

The legend of the willing burden bearer, *more commonly referred to as the parable of the second mile,* stems from a single line found in one of the oldest and most respected authorities on positive change ever written: the Bible.[28] Originally penned by a public tax collector-turned-transformation artist named Matthew, at the time this parable was first shared it was routine practice for a soldier to demand a citizen carry his load at least one Roman mile, a distance of one thousand paces.[29] This practice of ordering civilians to carry a heavy load was termed "impressment" and was certainly no easy task, especially considering that a soldier's backpack routinely weighed upwards of one hundred pounds.

History tells us that the Romans adopted the practice of impressment from the Persians, who were notorious for their cruelty to common citizens. In fact, the Persian version of impressment often forced civilians to carry a soldier's pack until they dropped. No limits were imposed on those with power. They were free to do as they wished. It was a brutal but intentional way of reminding everyone that the handful of people at the top, those with formal authority and status, could control those at the bottom.[30]

This punitive practice also served another very subtle but sinister purpose. Namely, it served as a means of promoting and protecting the status quo in order to preserve the existing social system of the day. In other words, it was designed to discourage those who didn't possess any special privilege, birthright, title, rank, or role from believing there was anything they could do to influence conditions for the better in the future—effectively enabling those with formal authority and status to intentionally keep those without any perceived positional power solidly trapped in the present mess they were in.

A Sinister Purpose

Unlike the Persians before them, the Romans did not want to incite the besieged population any more than they had to in order to maintain firm control. So they chose to limit the distance those in formal positions of authority could demand a citizen carry their load to a single mile. Less distance, but same intent—remind people who's in charge; promote the status quo; preserve the existing social system of the day.

It did not take long, however, for the people continually subjugated to this disempowering practice to learn exactly how far they had to extend to deliver the minimum required effort. In fact, citizens made it a routine practice to drive stakes into the ground precisely one mile from their homes. This way, when a soldier demanded their load be carried, the citizen would walk exactly to the next stake, set the pack down on the ground, and be finished. According to Roman law, the minimum requirement had been met.

Nobody expected more.

It was time for the soldier to grab his gear and move on.

So imagine a soldier's surprise when, at the obligatory mile marker, he stops and reaches for his heavy pack only to find that this particular citizen has chosen to keep walking.

This is when things get very interesting.

An Unconventional Response

The Roman soldiers of this era, the equivalents of today's *guardians of the status quo*, were accustomed to coercing people to do what they demanded. They surely didn't expect common citizens to think, much less act, on their own. Impressment was designed, after all, to be a tightly scripted, one-way transaction. Soldier demands; citizen complies.

Deviating from expectations not authorized.

You can't help but wonder then what must have been going through the soldier's mind when, after countless similar excursions in which previous citizens relished doing as little as possible to fulfill the task at hand, this one kept going.

"Is this some form of provocation?"

"Or perhaps the burden bearer is insulting my (the legionnaire's) strength?"

"Maybe he's just acting kindly toward me, a perceived enemy?"[31]

Although none of us can possibly know what the legionnaire was truly thinking in that moment, it's almost certain he never understood the burden bearer's true motivation. For in choosing to keep walking past the first mile marker toward the second, the citizen isn't choosing to kill the soldier with kindness. He's actually *seizing the initiative and taking back the power of choice*, turning the tables on both the soldier and the prevailing social order of the day in the process.

As it turns out, the way most of us have been taught to think about what it means to go the proverbial "extra mile" is incomplete and far less powerful than what this metaphor really has to offer. In reality, these words are not solely intended to persuade us to do more than required or extend further than expected. Rather, the legend of the willing burden bearer is meant to challenge each of us to do the unexpected by taking deliberate steps to say no to the status quo and yes to:

Thinking differently about our potential role in the world;
Acting boldly in shaping outcomes in our spheres of influence; and
Becoming the best version of ourselves possible by exercising the creativity of thought, diversity of   perspective, and depth of conviction to do what we can, when we can, where we can to try and make our part of the world a little better tomorrow than we found it today.

In taking the initiative to live what he believed, the willing burden bearer was demonstrating he would not allow himself to be bound by the confining, divisive, and demeaning practice of impressment. By his willingness to deviate from expectations in a manner that brought a little magic to the moment (in this case, unexpectedly carrying the tired soldiers load twice as far as the situation demanded), he chose to communicate in tangible terms his intent to live by different rules—rules consistent with his personal values—not the values being imposed on him by those around him.

Hence, the real message being conveyed in this timeless legend is that in a society where it's far more convenient and comfortable to blindly go where the path of societal norms lead us, we must be willing to set aside our fears and risk walking differently in the world. Providing us all with a compelling reminder how choosing to make a stand for what we what believe is worth fighting isn't merely some lofty ideal or overly ambitious objective reserved for a special few. It's a choice available to anyone. Anyone, that is, willing to act on the opportunities we encounter every day to guide, inspire, and be helpful in a way that intentionally does for others what we would like others to do for us—setting an example worth emulating along the way.

We Are the Choices We Make

As the almost two thousand year old legend of the willing burden bearer illustrates, leadership is more choice than chance; more disposition than position. It's about coming fully alive and accepting that the world in which we live is largely of our own making. We are, by the choices we routinely make, the primary architects of our realities.[32]

From the earliest days of recorded history, human beings have grappled with the reality of choice. Perhaps we struggle so much to decide if risking taking action is really worth it because we know we have to live with both the positive and negative effects of our choices. And as we have all likely experienced in our own lives, no one enjoys having to face the consequences of making poor choices.

NOTE

The world in which we live is largely of our own making... We are, by the choices we routinely make, the primary architects of our realities

Of course, it would certainly be easier to risk moving out in an uncommon or untried direction if we possessed the luxury of knowing in advance how things were going to turn out. After all, when we know the end of the story, what is there to fear? Maybe this is why so many of us like to read the last chapter of a book before we buy it. If we already know the ending, the odds are we're going to enjoy the journey that much more.

In our own lives, however, we don't possess the luxury of starting at the end and working our way backward. There is no DVR to skip the scenes we don't like. One of the unchangeable aspects of being human is that we have to do life in order: from front to back, beginning to end. No skipping parts, no jumping around. We've got to go scene by scene, experience by experience, and most importantly, opportunity by opportunity. And it is the choices we make, or fail to make for that matter, which construct the storyline we call our lives.

According to psychologist Rollo May, making choices is central to our identity and existence as human beings. "A man or woman becomes fully human only by his or her choices and his or her commitment to them. People attain worth and dignity by the multitude of decisions they make from day to day."[33] Leadership expert and former CEO Max DePree, commenting on the importance of choice in our lives as a means of attaining our fullest potential, affirms it is primarily through the choices we make that we distinguish ourselves from the masses and establish the foundation for a better future. In his book *Leading Without Power*, he writes, "To be without choices is a great tragedy, a tragedy leading to hopelessness and cynicism….Our choices after all *set us apart* and shape our legacy."[34] Something the willing burden bearer undeniably understood.

Here's why I'm confident making such a definitive statement. You see, in first-century Palestine, where the concept of going the extra mile finds its roots, the Romans had conquered much of the known world. One of the marvels of their conquest was a vast system of super highways, which they had built to and from their conquered territories. In fact, there were eventually over fifty-thousand miles of these roads spread throughout the empire, with each mile marked by a small stone indicating the distance to Rome.[35]

For the majority of citizens during that era subjected to the punitive practice of impressment, the mile markers represented the ability to be precise in doing *the minimum required effort*. In other words, they served as a visual reminder that mediocrity was acceptable as no one was expected to do any more than they had to. One mile, that's it; they were finished.

Task completed.

For the willing burden bearer, however, the mile markers symbolized something far different. Rather than viewing them as boundary markers designed to illustrate how little he could get away with doing, he chose to view them as *reference points* to demonstrate *how much more he was capable of doing*. Not to serve his own selfish purposes, but because he understood that the true measure of a life well lived is determined largely by how we choose to use *the opportunities* we have every day to help make the world around us a little better tomorrow than we found it today.

Parting Thoughts

On August 22, 2006, in a mine in the tiny southern African kingdom of Lesotho, a golf-ball-sized 603-carat diamond, subsequently named the "Lesotho Promise," was unearthed. The diamond, the biggest found in thirteen years and the fifteenth largest in the world, was described by gem experts as being of exceptional color quality and almost flawless.[36] Less than two months after it was found, the diamond was sold at auction in Antwerp, Belgium for $12 million—more than 3,870 times the tiny nation's per capita annual income.

Perhaps what's most interesting about this story is that the diamond wasn't found deep within the confines of the cavernous mine, buried under a mountain of rock and stone. It was unearthed in the most unlikely of areas: in a part of the cave frequented daily by the very workers hired to search for treasures just like these. No one knows how many people just missed stumbling upon this precious diamond before it was finally uncovered—a gem of immense value that had effectively remained *invisible in plain sight* for thousands of years, waiting to be discovered.

In the case of Mediocre Me, the treasure of immense value invisible in plain sight that I'm speaking of is the reservoir of positive potential waiting to be tapped within each and every one of us. Potential that can serve as *the fuel of change* at a time in our history when we desperately need more leaders who will reject mediocrity and risk modeling a more excellent way of being in the world—one opportunity at a time.

Chapter 4

Make Different, More Empowering Choices

*The history of free men is never really written
by chance, but by choice; their choice!*
—Dwight D. Eisenhower

Greece's history is replete with tales of heroes and the great battles they fought. Platea, Tangra, Coronea, and Chaeronea are but a handful of the battlefields that litter the small island nation. However, on a single spot marked by only a stark, white marble column in the middle of a grain field, you'll find arguably the most significant battlefield of all. It's a little-visited place called Leuctra, in the region of Boeotia, where in 371 BC General Epaminondas and his army from Thebes defeated the previously unconquerable army of Sparta.

It was a battle that forever altered Grecian history.

In Greek, Boeotia translates as "cow pasture," so essentially, Gen. Epaminondas and his armies vanquishing the most feared warriors in all of Greece was similar to the dairy farmers of Iowa marching on Washington, DC. It was simply too preposterous to consider.[37]

Which is why their story is so compelling.

You see, the Spartans were professional soldiers, and war was their business. As such, they were used to enslaving hundreds of thousands of people and took great pride in devastating their foes in battle. Conversely, the Boeotian people were more of a loose union of citizen farmers than they were professional fighters. And they differed from their adversaries in a more significant way. They rebelled against the predominate thinking of the time when it came to the rights they extended to their people.

In Boeotia, everyone was considered a full citizen of the state simply by virtue of their birthright. All were individually empowered to lead their own lives, capable of creating their own destinies, and encouraged to exercise responsibility to do their part to improve their country. By virtue of this broad sense of everyone's potential to influence outcomes, leadership was not reserved for a special few, but rather *was an opportunity afforded everyone.*[38]

WARNING
Passivity...does nothing but undermine our potential, destroy our families, damage our businesses, ruin our communities, and spoil our legacies

To the Spartans, however, citizenry and all its rights, liberties, and opportunities were extended only to certain classes. Power was the possession of the privileged. Coercion and compliance were the norm. The only real measure of an individual's worth in their society was someone's wealth, pedigree, or position, especially when it came to leadership.

The fact of the matter is, the Boeotians and Spartans could not have been more different.

In 371 BC, on the plains of Leuctra, Gen. Epaminondas and his army of free men squared off with the elite Greek warriors of Sparta, soundly defeating them in what to this day stands as one of the most unlikely victories in recorded military history. But that wasn't enough. You see, the citizen farmers insisted on pressing their advantage and taking the war to their enemy's front door—to the fabled city of Sparta itself.

And so they did.

What ensued was a series of battles that ultimately led to the Spartans' total defeat and, most importantly, resulted in the freeing of scores of Messenian slaves that had been doing the Spartan people's bidding for generations. The once-great nation of Sparta never fully regained its stature as a regional power. And, because of the collective efforts of an army of common people willing to accept personal responsibility for taking the initiative to lead the change they wanted to see, an empire built on oppression was finally brought to its knees.[39]

Revolution or Transformation

No matter how many times we encounter stories of courageous people like the Boeotian farmers-turned-warriors, who stretch beyond established boundaries or deviate from expected norms in order to benefit others, we are both encouraged and inspired. Seeing or hearing about those who exercise personal responsibility for helping those around them lead a better, fuller life, leaves us wanting to know more. Their willingness to break the mold of how many of us think about our ability to promote change in our surroundings certainly gets our attention.

It's interesting to note how the history of mankind is marked by two great forms of change: revolutionary and transformational. Both of which involve people making very different choices for the purpose of upending the status quo.

NOTE
The history of mankind is marked by two great forms of change: revolutionary and transformational

In times of social upheaval as we see in the courageous example of the Boeotians, the call for radical change frequently leads to resounding rhetoric and a compelling call to arms. The desire to change things suddenly and almost at any cost demands someone resort to violent or aggressive means to achieve a desired end, which reminds us revolutions strive to promote change in a particular system, society, or situation, *quickly*.[40]

Transformations, on the other hand, are much like evolution. That is, they are "time-released." Which means the process happens more slowly and deliberately. The dictionary tells us that "to transform" is "to

change in form, appearance, nature, or character, *usually for the better.*"[41]
The term "transformation" derives from the Greek word, *metamorphoo,*
which translates into the word "metamorphosis": a familiar phrase
that describes something or someone being changed into something
completely *different.*

In thinking about this concept, it's quite likely most of us will
think of a caterpillar transforming into a butterfly. And for good
reason, as few things in nature are as dramatic as watching an insect
once relegated to crawling its way through life one day suddenly
finding itself capable of flying freely. No longer encumbered by its
previous limitations, it has been liberated to show up in the world
differently.[42]

Hence, while revolutionary change is designed to bring about
instantaneous results, transformational change is more evolutionary in
nature. It reflects *a deliberate process* by which we choose to jettison old
ways of thinking and being so we can willingly push the boundaries of
our abilities and stretch the full extent of our capabilities so we can grow
into the best version of ourselves—one opportunity at time.

Transforming Intention into Action

It should be no surprise that the willingness to risk setting off in new,
unexplored directions is such a valued commodity in today's world. So
much so, in fact, that CEO's constantly rank creativity and innovation
as the most important leadership skill needed to successfully navigate the
present and smartly position for the future.[43]

If this is actually the case, however, why is it that research also
confirms creative people who dare to be different are rarely seen as
leaders? Could it be we've become so accustomed to a particular way
of thinking about leadership that we've lost sight of what it takes to be
truly exceptional?

In a 2011 study conducted by the Wharton Business School,
researchers set out to explore this important link between leadership
and innovation. What they discovered surprised them. Surveying both
employees at a multi-national corporation in India as well as college
students in the United States, they asked individuals to rate their

colleague's levels of creativity and leadership potential. In both cases, the most original and innovative people did not make the leadership list. After examining their findings, the lead author of the study speculated that the reason for these unexpected results is that "out-of-the-box-thinkers tend *not* to do the things that traditional leaders do, such as… *maintain the status quo…*"[44] As a result, they don't fit neatly into the often narrow way we've been encoded by our surroundings to routinely think about what constitutes leadership.

With this in mind, now consider the great transformations our own society has experienced, including the fight for American independence, the struggle for civil rights, the push for women's suffrage, the invention of the airplane, the advent of the television, and the explosion of the Internet. None of these materialized because everyone turned off their imaginations or believed the status quo should continue to exist unchallenged.

What each and every one of these milestones in history did have in common is that they began with someone willing to make the *choice to:*

> *Think differently* about their potential role in the world;
>
> *Act boldly* in shaping outcomes in their spheres of influence; and
>
> *Become the best version of themselves possible* by exercising the creativity of thought, diversity of perspective, and depth of conviction to try and make their part of the world a little better tomorrow than they found it today.

What I hope you take away from all this discussion about transformation is that none of the positive effects of the people's actions I mentioned were realized by fearing change or accepting mediocrity as the norm. Each of them was the result of someone first taking the risk to step out of their comfort zones and *make different, more empowering choices.* An insight meant to help us understand how effectively responding to the warnings occurring in our society doesn't demand that we start a revolution, but rather that we get busy transforming our good intentions into deliberate actions—one opportunity at a time.

Becoming Your Best You

Neuroscientists studying the human brain confirm that behind everything we do is a thought. Every behavior is motivated by a belief, and every action prompted by our attitude. This straightforward way of understanding how we choose to lead our lives is not a new phenomenon. In fact, long before psychologists, sociologists, and scientists understood this to be scientifically validated truth, it appeared in the Book of Proverbs. Over three thousand five hundred years ago we were told that people should "be careful how you think; your life is shaped by your thoughts."[45]

It was wise leadership advice then and remains wise advice today.

Now it's important to understand that when I refer to wisdom I'm doing so through the lens of cognitive psychology, which describes wisdom as the ability to make sound judgments, to learn from common experiences, and to conduct ourselves in ways that adds value into whatever it is we are doing. From such a view then, wisdom is less skill, trait, or ability than it is *a process*. Specifically, it is a process by which we consciously align our words, our ways, and our values so we can attempt to forge beauty out of the raw material of our lives. The Greeks called this ability *phronesis*, or practical wisdom.[46] A wisdom that equips us to do as the willing burden bearer did and use what we already know to go beyond what we currently think so we can lead our lives in a more excellent way.

>
> **NOTE**
> *The most profound changes we can make in our lives are not outward but inward*

What you will find in the remaining pages is a time-tested means to transform the willingness to reject mediocrity and embrace excellence as your preferred way of walking in the world into practical wisdom. The seven choices I share are mined from the same source as the legend of the willing burden bearer and represent inter-cultural, international, and intergenerational ways to maximize human potential by:

> Renewing your confidence
> Multiplying your influence
> Enhancing your motivation

Elevating your satisfaction

Increasing your effectiveness

Improving your relationships

Enriching your life

Perhaps more importantly, none of these choices require we possess any unique credentials, special training, minimum level of IQ, or particular type of personality in order to start putting them into use.

All we have to do is choose to get in the game.

As I've discovered so many times in my own personal leadership journey, the most profound changes we can make in our lives are not outward but inward: changes in how we think or feel, in what we value, and ultimately, in what we are willing to fight for. No one said striving to promote positive change in our surroundings is easy. But I'm here to remind you it is necessary. For as the great German poet, playwright, and philosopher Johann Wolfgang von Goethe once keenly remarked, "He who moves not forward goes backward."

Which begs the question: in which direction are you currently moving?

Parting Thoughts

One of my senior Air Force mentors is fond of saying, "The best leaders don't push for revolution, but instead seek to promote transformation." In other words, they are always looking for ways to transform present circumstances, no matter how daunting, into an opportunity to stretch and grow. Even, or perhaps I should say especially, if it means they have to challenge the status quo to do so.

As you'll recall from our earlier discussion, evolution implies adaption and growth, and neither occur by standing still. Forward progress demands we get comfortable pushing boundaries, treading new ground, and venturing into the unknown so we can evolve to be a little better tomorrow than we are today. But this process of personal transformation in which we enlarge our thinking so we can grow mentally; soften our heart so we can blossom spiritually; and grow our capacities so we can flourish and thrive individually and collectively, doesn't happen by accident.

It must be willful.

Much like the work that goes into building a muscular, well-defined physique, changing the way we think and act for the purpose of leading our lives in a more excellent way will take time. After all, nobody thinks in terms of developing strong biceps, or thighs, or any muscle for that matter, by lifting 9,000 pounds all at once. Instead, we lift fifty pounds for fifteen repetitions three times a week for a month. Same total amount of weight lifted—9,000 pounds—but accomplished slowly, deliberately. We schedule our workouts to give our body the time it needs to grow, and we keep at it, one choice to show up at a time. And, little by little, our physical body is transformed as we follow a regimen that builds muscle deliberately and increases our strength naturally.

So it is with becoming the best version of ourselves possible.

Remember, change always begins in our mind. The way we choose to think determines the way we feel and the way we feel influences the way we act. If we are filled with fear, we can't change much, and the status quo will continue to have its way with us. But if we are in control of our thinking, there is no limit to what we can do. Every problem, challenge, or obstacle we encounter is suddenly transformed into a character-building opportunity in disguise. The more difficult things are, the greater potential for building mental muscle and moral fiber—prompting each and everyone one of us to recognize we are already as much of a leader as we *choose* to be.

Part Two

THE CHOICES: TRANFORMING GOOD INTENTIONS INTO DELIBERATE ATTITUDES & ACTIONS

The manager accepts the status quo; the leader challenges it.
—Warren Bennis

What If?

"We cannot build our own future without helping others to build theirs."
—Bill Clinton

I'll admit I fell asleep in history class a few times. I remember one particular college professor lecturing at length about the British Corn Act of 1855 (or maybe it was some other vegetable he was talking about). Sure enough, minutes into his rambling I felt the fuzzy feeling that afflicts so many students of history begin to wash over me. My eyelids grew heavy, and before long, I was unconscious—an unwitting victim of BHA, Boring History Affliction.

But history need not always be so paralyzing. Enter counterfactual theory.

Counterfactual theory asks "what if" questions so we can speculate on how things would be different in the world if a particular event or action would not have occurred. For example, what if our founding fathers had not been so persistent in fighting for our freedom and independence? What if the Civil War was a draw? Or how would American society be different today if the Confederate army had prevailed or the United States had not gotten involved in World War I or II?

Here's my point. In every instance mentioned above, and countless others, the reason things turned out as they did is because someone was willing to acknowledge their fear but not be paralyzed by them. Instead of settling for the safety of the status quo and automatically accepting business as usual despite knowing there is a better way to be in the world, those who repeatedly have the greatest positive impact in their sphere of influence recognize the greatest opportunities for growth often occur when we are deeply uncomfortable. As a wise friend of mine once reminded me, "people will not change their situations until the pain of the present outweighs the fear of the future." His words affirming former first lady Eleanor Roosevelt's observation that "You gain strength, courage, and confidence by every experience in which you really stop to look fear in the face." To which I would simply add, *and choose to do as the willing burden bearer and keep walking forward anyway.*

So let me ask you a couple of "What If" questions of your own.

What if you routinely resisted the urge or pressure to settle for leading a life that is "good enough" and chose instead to risk pursuing excellence as your preferred way of being in the world? Or what if you decided to take a more expansive view of your potential and started writing a new, more empowering *personal leadership story* of your own? One which would allow you to discover for yourself that the only way you can expect to spur transformation in your surroundings is to first do the work to begin a transformation in yourself.

Of course, there is no way to know for certain how things might be different in your home, workplace, worship space, or community if you refused to allow a mediocre me mindset to convince you average is an acceptable way to lead your life. But I can tell you this much. Anything you do to follow the example of the willing burden bearer and consistently push the bounds of your abilities and stretch the full extent of your capabilities will bring you one step closer to living a life of true purpose, meaning, and significance.

And the best part is all you have to do to get started is begin making different, more empowering choices. Choices which can transform ordinary encounters into extraordinary opportunities to guide, inspire, and be helpful in a way that willfully does for others what you would like others to do for you by setting an example worth emulating—one opportunity at a time.

The First Choice

Take Risks...
Be Proactive

*There are risks and costs to action. But they are far
less than the long-range risks of comfortable inaction.*
—John F. Kennedy

Chapter 5

Be the First Penguin

Following the herd is a sure way to mediocrity.
—Patti Wilson

Not long ago I had the opportunity to don a penguin costume and jump into a pool of icy-cold water, all in the name of supporting a good cause. I, and about three dozen others, braved near-zero temperatures to take turns diving into a frosty pool (really an extra-large refuse dumpster) to help raise money for the Special Olympics.

Although it seemed like a fun idea when I first volunteered, I have to admit I was a little fearful the actual day of the event. Now don't get me wrong. I very much enjoyed searching for and buying the penguin costume and had a great time driving to the event, flippers on the wheel and oversized orange penguin feet on the pedals. But as I turned into the parking lot and saw the ambulance parked in front of the diving platform, I seriously began questioning what I had signed up for.

Fortunately, I brought my teenage son, Taylor, with me, so any chances of making a quick getaway were quickly met with a "don't be weak, Dad" comment. Admittedly, about that time I thought about Shakespeare's words in *King Henry IV:* "Discretion is the better part of valor." In other words, it is often better to think carefully and not act than to do something that may later cause some very real problems.

In this case, the problem I was worried about was catching pneumonia or, worse, getting a chance to take a post-dive ambulance ride after my heart stopped beating due to the shock of encountering the frigid water. Although far-fetched, it's funny what your mind will do when you're scantily clothed in a penguin outfit in below-freezing temperatures waddling across the parking lot to jump into a refuse dumpster-turned-diving pool.

Needless to say, my desire to offer someone else the penguin suit to wear so they could take the plunge for me, or make up an excuse why I couldn't carry through with my jump, was inviting, but ultimately not the right thing to do.

So there I stood, perched on the launching pad overlooking the frostiest water I've ever seen. With people watching, cameras rolling, and my stomach churning, I think I understood what it must feel like to be "the first penguin."

I remember coming across the idea of the "first penguin" in the late Randy Pausch's book *The Last Lecture.* Paush, a former professor at Carnegie Mellon, describes how he developed a "First Penguin Award" to reward students who took great risks in pursuing their goals, even though they met with failure. The title of the award comes from the notion that when penguins are about to jump into water that might contain predators, well, somebody's got to be the first to jump. The First Penguin award is, in essence, a celebration of risk taking.

What Is Risk Taking?

What, exactly, is a risk? Risks are difficult to define because they are often in the eye of the beholder. For some people, driving a motorcycle is risky. For others, investing in the stock market or committing to a serious relationship is a frightening and risky endeavor.

Risks then are those things that make us feel challenged beyond our usual comfort zone. Risk-taking pushes us into areas of "uncertainty" and puts us to the test. It moves us from the safety of the "known" and forces us in the direction of the unknown. In terms of overcoming a mediocre me mindset, I've come to define risk taking as *the willingness to be different where different can get things moving in a new, more empowering direction.*

You'll very likely note this definition of risk taking implies

NOTE
Risk taking is *the willingness to be different where different can get things moving in a new, more empowering direction*

a bias for action. It demands you move outside the narrow confines of the status quo, abandoning business as usual in order to do something uncommon. It requires you possess, in a word, *nerve.*

Much like the brave penguin that commits to being the first to plunge headfirst into the uncharted water before him, possessing the nerve to venture in a direction others fear is the stuff of pioneers. Maybe that's why those willing to risk undertaking an action in order to achieve a desirable goal can be counted by the handful rather than the herd. Their openness to breaking out of old routines and deviating from the conventional pathway pursued by the masses certainly isn't easy as it presents a clear potential for failure.

Fear of Failure

As I shared earlier, fear of failure is one of the single greatest hurdles anyone will face in their quest to lead their lives in a more excellent way. The difference, however, between those who press forward to achieve something and those cemented in place by the perceived safety of the status quo lies in the willingness to take the first step; to risk making the proverbial leap of faith in a new direction—to commit to either remaining paralyzed by the potential of what could go wrong, or energized by the possibilities of what can go right.

One choice breaks us while the other builds us.

I'll always remember the day I came across a solitary framed piece of paper hanging on the wall of my friend Max Lucado's study. It was a short, simple letter from a publisher, accepting his first manuscript for publication. Since that time, Max has gone on to sell over eighty million books and is considered one of the most successful inspirational authors in history.

However, what struck me the most as I read the first of what would become a steady stream of acceptance letters was what I knew the piece of paper symbolized for Max. You see, this was not Max's first letter from a publisher, but rather his fifteenth. The first fourteen publishers had rejected him. But Max, committed to pursuing his dream and undeterred by apparent failure, kept sending out manuscripts. And time has revealed the world is a better place for his doing so.

NOTE
To risk failure is to embrace living life to its fullest

Sadly, too many potential leaders in our world don't make the choice to face their fears head on. Instead of possessing the tenacity to keep pressing toward the second mile marker when times are toughest, they do what's safe and stop at the first, sacrificing the growth that would have come from enduring adversity along the way. And as a result of their one-mile mindset, they quickly reach a plateau. Stagnation sets in and forward progress stops in their journey to become the best versions of themselves.

If only they better understood what they were missing.

The truth is, to risk failure is to embrace living life to its fullest. Failure, and its close cousin adversity, are like the hammer and anvil of the blacksmith. They work together to shape the yet-unformed steel of your character into something strong, durable, and resilient. Both the pounding of the hammer and the strength of the anvil are needed to forge you into the kind of leader you want to be and those around you deserve to see—a leader willing to risk doing what needs to be done, no matter how daunting or difficult the goal at hand.

Thus, like the penguin that has to be the first to test the waters for predators, risk taking always involves the possibility of failure or an unpleasant outcome. Otherwise it wouldn't be risky! Thus, the important point to remember is that becoming a successful risk taker isn't measured by how often you take a chance and actually succeed. Rather, it is learning to acknowledge your fears and not allow yourself to be paralyzed by them.

Risk Taking: Key to Progress

For those of us who serve in the military, risk taking is not anything new. In fact, it is ingrained throughout our history. During World War II, General George C. Marshall was promoted to General of the Army, making him the highest ranking military officer in America. Despite never having commanded even at the division level, this brilliant leader became the primary architect of the now famous D-Day invasion in Normandy, France—an operation fraught with risk. Persisting against numerous objections from those who questioned his credibility to organize such an effort, as well as those who were convinced such a bold, daring plan would result in unacceptable losses, Gen. Marshall remained convinced the invasion was a risk worth taking. And today we know he was right, as his successful plan was the catalyst that sparked the end to the protracted conflict in Europe.[48]

Of course, risk taking is by no means limited to the military. In fact, many of the world's most successful sports stars take risks all the time. For example, Mario Andretti is arguably the most famous name associated with professional car racing. He's won races all over the world, including the European Grand Prix and the Indianapolis 500. For all those who have seen Andretti race, especially those he has competed against, what stands out above all else is his tenacity in pursuing bold, aggressive moves. For Andretti, pushing the envelope of his own abilities and his cars' capabilities remain hallmarks of his performances. The willingness to take risks is what enables him to stretch ever closer to achieving his full potential.

Beyond military leaders and sports figures, risk taking also plays a prominent role in politics. In fact, history is filled with examples of risk taking by political leaders that have resulted in major benefits for their countries. One has only to remember the Berlin Airlift during the Truman years, President Reagan's challenge to Communism that resulted in the "fall" of the Berlin Wall, or the late Pakistani Prime Minister Benazir Bhutto's ascent to her country's highest political post as the first woman elected to lead a Muslim state in modern history, which subsequently paved the way for others to follow suit.[49]

As all these successful leaders affirm, risk taking isn't about being reckless, forging forward without thought of where you're going or what you're doing. Rather, it's about having the confidence in yourself to make one risky choice at a time. Recognizing that as you take a calculated risk and learn from it, whether you succeed or fail, your confidence will grow and risk taking will be just a bit easier the next time—testimony to how each risky step you take in a new direction stretches you beyond what you've known so you can embrace the possibilities of what can be learned from venturing into the unknown…even when the path ahead is obscured, uncertain, or unexplored.

Changing the World…One Risk at a Time

While military leaders, sports stars, and politicians certainly provide us with compelling examples of the importance of taking risks, it's often the experiences of cutting-edge business entrepreneurs that capture our imagination the most.

Take the story of the late Apple Computers co-founder Steve Jobs.

Jobs started a billion-dollar business in his garage in his early twenties at a time when the personal computer business didn't even exist. He went on to lead the field in four separate industries: music, with his development of the revolutionary iPod; movies, with his development of Pixar, one of the world's most successful animation studios; personal computing, with his Apple brand of products whose trendy design and ease of use is legendary; and, most recently, his company's introduction of the iPhone and iPad have once again transformed the way people communicate and left an indelible mark on the world.

NOTE
Risk taking isn't about being reckless, forging forward without thought of where you're going or what you're doing

As a result of Steve Jobs's propensity for taking risks, millions are now employed in the computer industry. And, perhaps more than anyone else, Jobs brought digital technology to the masses. As a visionary willing to follow the example of the first penguin and venture into previously unexplored territory, he saw that computers could be much more than drab productivity tools. Instead, he believed they could help unleash human creativity and enhance enjoyment, and as a result, he consistently pushed the envelope in order to design, develop, and deliver elegant products that capture consumers' imagination. As Shawn Levy wrote in his 1994 book, *Insanely Great,* Jobs was "the most passionate leader one could hope for, a motivating force without parallel." A man committed to changing the world, one risk at a time.

Maybe it should be no surprise that Steve Jobs's high-risk approach to business stemmed from his personal philosophy on life. This philosophy was captured in a single question he used to ask himself every time he was faced with making an important choice: "*What would I do if this was the last night of my life?*" It's a thought-provoking inquiry that invariably provided Steve Jobs with the passion and courage to take bold steps in an unknown direction. And it leaves us too ask ourselves what would we do differently, if we to only had one more contribution to make in the fleeting adventure we call life?

Parting Thoughts

There is a quote on the wall of Apple's headquarters in Palo Alto, California, that for me seems to serve as the perfect creed for the world's eyes-wide-open, risk-taking leaders willing to walk differently in the world. Here's what it says:

> Here's to the crazy ones. The misfits. The rebels. The troublemakers. The round pegs in the square holes. The ones who see things differently. They're not fond of rules. And they have no respect for the status quo. You can quote them, disagree with them, glorify or vilify them. About the only thing you can't do is ignore them. Because they change things. They push the human race forward. And while some may see them as the crazy ones, we see genius. Because the people who are crazy enough to think they can change the world are the ones who do.

How many times have you held back from trying something new because you were afraid of how others would perceive you if you failed? Or, how many times have you been in a classroom or a meeting and didn't share ideas because you were afraid of sounding uneducated or unsophisticated? Maybe you've even found yourself holding back from ordering something new from a menu for fear of being disappointed. Any way you look at it, when we are afraid to risk making mistakes, the only outcome that is guaranteed is that we won't get very far in life.

Time and time again as a leader I've found that one of the best approaches to risk taking is to try many different things on a small scale, test them in practice, and then assess what works and doesn't work before I press forward any further. By pushing this cycle of "prudent experimentation," I satisfy my innate desire to constantly stretch and grow while minimizing the chance I'll extend into something I cannot recover from, personally or professionally.

One of the most wonderful things about children, and I believe there are many, is that they are not unnecessarily burdened by the fear of trying new things. In fact, what I've found is that kids don't consider failure a bad thing. For that matter, they don't even interpret it as failure. Rather, falling short of achieving their objective in the moment is a tool for learning. In their minds, it is little more than an opportunity for them, in the words of industrialist Henry Ford, "to begin again, this time more intelligently."

Maybe some of us grown-ups would do well to more frequently choose to adopt a similar mindset.

Chapter 6

Risk Going First

*Only those who will risk going too far
can possibly find out how far one can go.*
—T. S. Eliot

Admittedly, many of the examples I've shared with you throughout these pages have been dramatic stories of leaders whose bold actions and willingness to remain undaunted by failure have paid off in big ways on the world stage. The fact remains, however, that the greatest reservoir of potential to promote positive change in our world isn't found in the select few whose names and accomplishments adorn history books or whose efforts have resulted in the establishment of a multi-billion dollar businesses. Rather, it is waiting to be tapped within the multitude of leaders like you and me who are open to leading their lives in a more excellent way—right where we are today.

Take Roger Olian, for example.

On January 13, 1982, in the midst of a severe snowstorm, Air Florida Flight 90 crashed immediately after takeoff into the 14th Street Bridge that spans the Potomac River in Washington, DC.

All but five people of the jet's seventy-nine passengers and crew members immediately perished in the crash.[50]

Many federal offices in downtown Washington had closed early the day of the accident in response to quickly developing blizzard conditions. Thus there was a massive backup of traffic on almost all of the city's roads, making it very difficult for rescue crews and ambulances to reach the crash location. As rescuers arrived at the site, they quickly discovered they were unable to assist those passengers in the water, as they did not have adequate equipment to reach them. To make matters worse, below-freezing temperatures and heavy ice made swimming out to them all but impossible.

Multiple attempts to throw makeshift lifelines to the survivors proved ineffective.

As the small handful of survivors thrashed about in the deadly water below, media crews from Washington, DC's major TV and radio stations captured all that was occurring. Frame by frame, moment by moment, the tragic fate of Flight 90 was broadcast in homes across the nation. People everywhere watched and waited, hoping and praying the few survivors could be plucked from the near-frozen river before they too were claimed by the icy grave.

CAUTION:
Regret is both an emotion as well as a punishment we administer to ourselves

As rescue workers struggled to find ways to try to save the people from the river below, one man, Roger Olian, a sheet-metal foreman at a Washington hospital for the mentally ill, was on his way home across the 14th Street Bridge when he heard someone yelling there was an aircraft down in the water. Without hesitation, he jumped into the frigid river to try to do what he could for those in need below.

Within a minute, Olian made contact with one of the survivors and guided them to the nearby shoreline. With ice sticking to his body, people asked him not to try again, but he would have nothing of it. With no regard for his own comfort or well being, he continued to go back until he was assured everyone was safe. It was only then that he finally made his way back to the edge of the river, where he collapsed, partly from exhaustion and partly from hypothermia.

In making the choice that blistery winter afternoon to risk his own safety for the benefit of the small handful of crash survivors, Roger Olian accepted responsibility to lead the effort to help those unable to help themselves. His taking the plunge into the unknown frozen waters below reminds us that leadership isn't a matter of possessing a particular rank, title, or position, but instead it's about taking proactive action to do something to positively influence outcomes— be it from the front, the middle, the back, or, as in Roger Olian's case, even from a bridge.

The Risk Blocker: Fear of Regret

Who can't help but be inspired by the amazing story of an ordinary person like Roger Olian? Unafraid to risk his own safety and well being to help total strangers in need, his positive example prompts us to ponder what we would do if we unexpectedly found ourselves facing similar circumstances.

Have you considered what it is that holds you back in life from taking risks? Not necessarily extraordinary bridge-jumping-size risks on a frigid day into a half-frozen lake like Roger Olian, mind you, but any risk? You may be surprised to hear that our propensity to avoid risk-taking is largely a function of how our brains try to protect us from our very human fear of experiencing *regret*.

Of course, we've all encountered regret firsthand. We experience it as everything from that sinking feeling we get when we realize we should have known better, that subtle sadness that comes from reflecting on past mistakes, and that deep yearning we develop to undo what's already happened. It's wishing we could get a second chance. Hence, regret is both an emotion as well as a punishment we administer to ourselves. It prompts us to believe that it's

NOTE
Risk taking is the price we must be willing to pay to get things moving in a new, more empowering, direction

better to stick with what's safe, predictable, and controllable than to take a bold leap in a new, unknown direction.

Not surprisingly, our desire to avoid regret also stems from our innate discomfort with change. Our dread of making an improper choice convincing us inaction is a suitable, if not altogether preferable, response to risking an outcome we cannot fully control.

But the fact of the matter is, anyone trying to avoid regret just won't get very far in life. Progress, as we've undoubtedly experienced ourselves, is often marked by the scrapes, bumps, and bruises, physically, mentally, and emotionally, that come from trying something different for the purpose of making a positive difference in our spheres of influence. And though the circumstances may vary, the law of risk remains unchanged: risk taking is the price we must be willing to pay to *get things moving in a new, more empowering, direction.*

Of course, learning this lesson for ourselves means we have to risk our own version of bridge jumping. It's scary to dive in to do what needs to be done when we can't guarantee we won't experience regret. But often, taking leaps in a new and bold direction is the only way we can discover what we are really capable of achieving. Let me share a bridge-jumping story of my own to help make my point.

His Helping Hands

A little more than a decade ago, our family was transferred to a base in Wichita, Kansas, where I assumed duties as a tanker aircraft squadron commander. Our family found a nice home not far from the base and went about getting settled into the community.

One of the first things we did was locate a wonderful church, which just happened to be mere minutes from our house. Shortly after joining the congregation we began to get involved in one of the many service efforts the church offered as a way to try and make a positive difference in the lives of those in the community. In this case, it was a program called His Helping Hands, which distributed food, clothing, and household goods and appliances to people in need of assistance. Everyone was welcome; no one was turned away.

His Helping Hands was run by a small cadre of wonderful volunteers out of an old warehouse facility several miles from the church. The building was, well, what you would expect from an old warehouse. But, despite being poorly lit, having no heat or air conditioning (remember, it's Kansas), and slightly small for our needs, we made it work. After all, the budget was tight, the price was right, and everything we might have had in a better building was more than made up for by the amazing dedication of the small army of selfless volunteers. They braved snowstorms, heat waves, and everything in between do what they could, when they could, where they could to bring some measure of comfort, compassion, and companionship to all those who walked through those old rusty doors looking for a hand up in their time of need.

So where's the risk in this story, you ask? Well, here you go.

After being part of this effort for almost a year, I saw the need and heard the talk of how nice it would be to have a bigger, newer facility that would allow us to expand the services we provided the community into such areas as free medical and dental checkups, job training, an expanded food pantry, and a host of other initiatives. I started thinking about what could be done to see the compelling vision of an expanded His Helping Hands program come to life. One Friday night, while a group of us were enjoying a late dinner at the facility, an idea came to mind that I subsequently (and literally) scribbled onto a napkin and, for whatever reason, chose to share at that very moment with those around me. The plan (if you can call a spaghetti-stained napkin drawing a plan) involved raising funds to erect a new twenty-eight thousand square foot expandable warehouse facility on the seventeen acres someone had generously donated to the church directly across the street from our current location.

But here's the twist.

I proposed the project be funded using an unexpected and untraditional strategy. Instead of asking for donations from the congregation, we would raise all the money via a combination of constructing a service-celebration park on the new His Helping Hands campus with every brick, tree, and bench funded (and etched) with the contributor's name. We would also host an art auction and engage several national foundations in providing a matching grant for every dollar we raised via the park construction and art auction project. The group loved the idea, and I offered to transfer my napkin plan to paper so they could circulate the idea to the church leadership. But then they threw in their own unexpected twist. They not only wanted me to plan and lead the effort, they wanted me to sell the plan to the church leadership—all sixty of the elders. Oh, but wait, there's another little fact I need to add. They asked me to do so knowing that several previous proposals to expand this program had been rejected. The batting average to date for all other attempts was a noteworthy .000. And if that wasn't intimidating enough, I had never conducted a fundraiser of this magnitude before, I was a professional military officer and aviator and not a businessman, and I knew only one person on the church leadership board (with a majority approval required to proceed). It suffices to say I began to experience regret just for mentioning the idea.

Despite feeling woefully inadequate and outright fearful of experiencing not only the potential rejection of my plan by the board, but also outright failure if the effort stalled or didn't raise the capital to see the effort through, I knew it was the right thing to do. So I took the leap and did my research, built a business plan, created a presentation, and scheduled a meeting with the church leadership—all sixty of them.

In short, what happened next was nothing short of miraculous. Here's the high-speed version. I gave my pitch to the group, which they unanimously approved. They had one condition: I would have to lead the effort and present the effort to the congregation, and they would take care of submitting applications for the matching grants, as well as developing all the materials required to promote the campaign. Now mind you, my whole life I've been pew-bound. Meaning, I'd never spoken in front of a large church body before. Or any church body, for that matter. But a deal was a deal. I got to work with my team, and in a matter of months, we transformed a spaghetti-stained napkin plan into a successful campaign that raised in excess of $500,000. And today, His Helping Hands, all twenty-eight thousand square feet of it, is touching lives in amazing ways in Wichita, Kansas. This living testimony to risk-taking serves as a tangible reminder that often our fondest memories are the by-product of our willingness to face our fear of experiencing regret head on by taking a bold leap in an unknown or uncertain direction.

Regrets of Action versus Regrets of Inaction

Andy Stanley, in his book *The Next Generation Leader*, says that "generally speaking, you are probably never going to be more than 80 percent certain. Waiting for greater certainty may cause you to miss an opportunity."

Acting on opportunities to build value into others' lives, be it as Roger Olian did on that blistery winter day in Washington, DC, or in transforming an idea into reality like the reinvented His Helping Hands program, is risky. And there is nothing easy about taking risks—if for no other reason than every time we venture outside our comfort zones and deviate from the status quo, we open ourselves up to experiencing regret. But here's a little secret. Scientists tell us there are two forms of regret. One, *regret of inaction*, is based on what we fail to do when action is warranted. The other, *regret of action*, is the result of what we have chosen to do. Inaction regrets leave us wondering how things in our lives or our surroundings would be different if we had, in fact, acted when we had the opportunity to do so; action regrets leave us reflecting on what we would do different if we could rewind the tape and try again. Although both may have consequences in the short term, it turns out one choice leaves a far deeper negative imprint on us for the long term.

Social psychologists confirm that although we tend to pay more attention to action regrets in the short term, when people look across their lives as a whole, it's the inaction regrets we remember most. *More than five times as much, in fact.*[51] I can tell you now that had I not stepped up to see the napkin plan for His Helping Hands come to

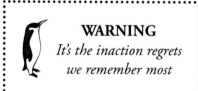

WARNING
It's the inaction regrets we remember most

life, there would now be a very significant regret of inaction in my life. And although I certainly have a whole pile of action regrets I'd like to get a "do-over" on, I can say every one of these has presented an opportunity for growth personally, professionally, or spiritually. Each risky action I've chosen to take afforded me the chance to both improve as a person and as a leader, just for having tried something different.

So now the question is, what precautions can we all take to inoculate ourselves against the enemy of growth we call "inaction regret?" I'd suggest you start by making little bets.

The concept of little bets stems from Peter Sims' work describing how big breakthroughs in life start *by making small, deliberate moves in a different direction*. In simple terms, little bets are those small actions we take to push the bounds of our current realities. Grounded in cutting-edge research exploring human creativity and innovation, Sims chronicled how the greatest achievements, be it in our personal or professional lives, business, government, or any industry for that matter, rarely result from making big, bold, "all or nothing" plays. Rather, real progress, progress that is sustainable, repeatable, and scalable, is most often a byproduct of abandoning a mediocre me mindset and testing the waters of change deliberately and consistently, one small initiative at a time.[52]

Take the founding of online social networking and microblogging sensation Twitter, for example.

Twitter originated out of a little bet made by a company called Odeo, a podcasting outfit with little to no name recognition, no significant market share, and sagging revenues. In other words, the company was going nowhere fast. But it did possess one novel idea: to develop a platform to send short messages to scores of people quickly and simultaneously. So following a now-famous day-long brainstorming session, the Odeo team agreed to make a little bet and step out in a new direction by test marketing their novel approach to bring people together via digital messaging. And the rest is literally history.

The willingness of the founders of Odeo to think differently and act boldly in setting off in a previously unexplored direction led to the creation of a sensation that to this day has over 500 million active users generating over 340 million tweets a day. And it didn't happen by accident. They changed the world of social networking not because they feared change, but because they were unafraid to stretch their capacities and expand their capabilities in order to demonstrate their commitment to becoming the best version of themselves possible.

Parting Thoughts

Much of the progress we've experienced in our world has been driven by well-known risk takers such as Gen. George Marshall, Mario Andretti, Harry S. Truman, Ronald Reagan, Benazir Bhutto, and Steve Jobs. However, risk taking is not limited military leaders, sports heroes, politicians, or entrepreneurs. Instead, it is the purview of all those who, like the brave first penguin, have set aside their fear of failure and taken the plunge into untested waters. Leaders like Max Lucado, Roger Olian, and the innovators at Odeo who choose to operate in the spirit of the willing burden bearer by *being different when different can get things moving in a new, more empowering direction.*

Remember, you learn to overcome your fear of change by becoming more comfortable taking risks. The more risks you take, the less fear can have its way with you. But risk taking need not be particularly dramatic or profoundly ambitious. You don't need to jump off a bridge or into a refuse dumpster-turned-diving pool to prove you're a person with a bias for action. Instead, it can be as simple as risking to continue forward with a difficult project when the going gets tough and you seem to be stuck. Or, it can be choosing to acknowledge that sometimes the riskiest thing you can do as a leader—be it in your home, workplace, worship space, or community—is to step aside and let someone else's idea or program take priority over your own.

Thinking back to that frigid afternoon when I was scantily clad in my penguin costume preparing to jump into the extra-large refuse dumpster turned diving pool, I'm reminded that, although I did not have to worry about predators lurking in the icy water below me, I did wonder for a moment if what I was about to do really made good sense. It was then, however, that I realized by setting aside my own small fears in order to carry out this gesture for a cause I believed in that I was living out my personal commitment to try and grow into the best version of myself possible not just in words, but in lifestyle.

For in donning the penguin suit and taking that frigid plunge that day, I was reminded how venturing into the unknown, although scary, can help awaken the senses. It provides us a precious opportunity to feel more alive and engaged than we might have ever felt before. The willingness to set aside our fears of experiencing inaction regret compels us to take the initiative and accept responsibility for leading the change we want to see—one bold leap at a time.

Author Seth Godin once remarked that there are two kinds of mistakes people are prone to make in life. There is the mistake of overdoing the defense of the status quo, the error of investing too much time and energy in keeping things as they are. And then there are the mistakes we make while doing something to try and invent the future we dream of—the error of small experiments gone bad.

Though we are almost never hurt by the second kind of mistake, we persist in making the first kind, again and again.

As I close this chapter, let me leave you with one final short story I recently read in a book by Gail Sheehy who recounts her experience interviewing a number of people in their eighties and nineties, asking them a simple but profound question: "As you look back on your life, do you believe it has been worthwhile?" One man's response jumped out to me from all the others. "I always toed the straight and narrow line in my life," he shared. "I always did what I was supposed to do, even if it didn't match what I wanted to do. I never took any risks in my life. And now you ask if my life has been worthwhile. I tell you, I feel as if I never lived it."[53]

> **NOTE**
> *You learn to overcome your fear of change by becoming more comfortable taking risks. The more risks you take, the less fear can have its way with you*

I don't know about you, but I surely don't want to fall into this same trap of one day looking back over my life and feeling as though, because I never risked stretching my abilities or testing the extent of my capabilities, I failed to really live.

All the more reason why I believe we should constantly be on the lookout for opportunities to go first, to show and go the way in creating the kind of world we all desire and deserve—even if it means risking being called crazy, misfit, rebel, troublemaker, or round peg in square hole in the process.

The Second Choice

MODEL THE CHANGE YOU WANT TO SEE... BE RESPONSIBLE

"We need role models who are going to break the mold."
—Carley Simon

Chapter 7

Be the Difference
You Want to See

First say to yourself what you would be; and then do what you have to do.
—Epictetus

Years ago an elementary school teacher chose to make a special video to share with her first-grade class. The video was shot in a school playroom filled with toys young kids absolutely love. One of the toys was an inflated Bobo the Clown doll, a long-time favorite with the children, which stood almost as tall as the first graders themselves. Next to Bobo was a large plastic baseball bat.

During one of her lunch hours, the teacher filmed one particular little boy in the playroom who was having fun with Bobo. In fact, she made it a point to encourage the little boy to use the plastic bat to inflict some serious damage to the unsuspecting (and innocent, I might add) plastic clown. So the little boy gladly obliged and began whacking Mr. Bobo like it was a professional baseball homerun derby.

Bobo proceeded to have a bad day. The little boy had a great time. And the teacher got it all on film.

Now here's where things get really interesting.

The teacher took her newly recorded video to one of her other first-grade classes the next day and played it for the children before they went to the playroom for a little recreation. It showed lots of kids playing with a host of toys, but it also featured the young boy providing a pounding to a defenseless Mr. Bobo. The teacher never said a word; she just showed the film and then escorted the kids into the recreation room so they could play.

So what do you think happened next?

The kids, boys and girls alike, made a beeline for the bat and began giving the inflated clown a series of relentless beatings. Applying what they'd seen on the tape, it turned out to be another bad day for Mr. Bobo.

And again, the teacher caught it all on film.[54]

This study, though humorous, proved something we already innately know. *Modeling* is one of the most powerful ways we can influence others, for good or bad.[55]

Rethinking the Power of Our Actions

I have to admit that every time I think about this story of Bobo, I can't help but smile. The mental visual of these young, innocent, and even (seemingly) angelic children pummeling a defenseless inflated clown reminds me of when I was in elementary school. You see, as a kid I also got a lot of practice swinging that plastic bat, as I too was once a Bobo beater. I modeled the same behaviors I saw my classroom pals routinely put into practice.

Today, many years later, the important part of this story has nothing to do with Bobo. It simply but effectively illustrates just how much attention we pay to what other people are *doing*. And although from an early age we are taught that a role model is someone whose behavior is routinely imitated by others, few people understand there's more to role modeling than first meets the eye.

> **NOTE**
> *Role modeling is actually our preferred means of empowering ourselves and those around us to reject mediocrity and stretch ourselves in new directions*

The magic of role modeling is that it works at any age, in any place, and at any time. As human being possess a natural tendency to want to make things easier when facing the discomfort associated with change, role modeling actually helps alleviate this burden as sociologists confirm the *first* place we look to determine how we should respond when facing unfamiliar circumstances is to *others*. In fact, we not only routinely learn what to do by watching those around us, we also learn what not to do, when to do it, and what to expect when we do it.[56]

Thus, it turns out role modeling is actually our *preferred means of empowering ourselves and those around us to reject mediocrity and stretch ourselves in new directions.* Why? Because:

- Someone else is already doing it (it's safe);
- I can see what they're doing (it's visible); and
- I don't need to think for myself when I can just emulate what someone else is doing (it's easy).

Albert Bandura, one of the world's most prominent social psychologists and originator of the original Bobo experiment, helps us understand why this is: "Learning would be exceedingly laborious, not to mention hazardous, if people had to rely solely on the effects of their own actions to inform them what to do."[57] In watching others, we form our own ideas that will later become our basis for guiding what we choose to do, or not do.

Intuitively, of course, we know role modeling has a powerful influence on us the same way that the Bobo-beating children knew to pick up the bat and begin beating on the plastic clown after watching a video of one of their classmates doing the very same thing.[58] And as researchers have repeatedly validated who we are and what we become are not just functions of our own direct experiences. They are very much a byproduct of the perceived or actual consequences of what we routinely see emulated by someone else.

Our example, it turns out, is the most powerful way to demonstrate and communicate our commitment to leading our lives in a more excellent way, each and every day.

Need more proof?

NOTE

Sociologists tell us that even the most introverted person in the world will influence at least 10,000 people in their lifetime

Sociologists tell us that even the most introverted person in the world will influence at least 10,000 people in their lifetime.[59] No matter who you are, where you work, or what title, position, rank, or role you possess, you will leave your mark, for good or bad, on scores of people. And if that fact isn't significant enough for you, scientists using special brain-imaging technology have proven we begin having an impact on others in the initial 1/20th of a second of an encounter.

We can't even think that fast![60]

The Powerful Role of Modeling

I am blessed with a wonderful family. As a father of two energetic and gifted young men I want to see grow into their full potential, I am very much aware that my example is central to their healthy development: psychologically, emotionally, and spiritually.

Psychologists and sociologists tell us that the more we identify with the person we are watching or the more connected we are to them emotionally, the more likely their actions will have a particularly strong influence on our own behavior. But these same scientists are quick to point out that we also experience a similar emotional connection when we are exposed to the selfless, courageous, and heroic *examples* of others. This helps to explain why we are so prone to take notice of those leaders who, though operating far outside our immediate circle of family and friends, demonstrate the positive attitudes and actions we want to possess and likely, even emulate ourselves. Take Roger Staubach, for example.

Staubach, in addition to being a Hall-of-Fame quarterback for the Dallas Cowboys from 1969 to 1979, has consistently chosen to be different for the purpose of making a positive difference in his surroundings. After completing a remarkable career in the NFL, Staubach has gone on to become a very successful businessman and generous philanthropist who chooses to run his charity foundation far differently than many athletes and celebrities do today. Instead of soliciting donations, throwing fundraising parties, or seeking publicity, nearly every dollar given away comes out of his pocket. "If you have a charity, it's very instrumental that you put your own wealth into it," Staubach remarked in a recent interview.[61] In fact, Staubach and his wife are so committed to building value into others' lives that, as part of their will, a very large portion of their assets have been bequeathed to their nonprofit so they can continue to make a lasting difference in the world long after they are gone.

Roger Staubach, in my view, represents the positive qualities you'd want in a friend, parent, and leader. He's committed, courageous, dependable, and generous. Decades after he quit playing football, I still look to Roger Staubach as someone whose example is worth emulating.

Now that's impact. And it's why role modeling is so important and powerful at any and every stage of our lives.

Brain Turbulence

I expect right about now that some of you reading this will be thinking how it's certainly easier to advocate for deviating from the status quo and modeling a better way of being in the world than it is to actually take the first bold (and admittedly scary) step to actually do it. And to be fair, I'd be the first to admit that you're right. After all, it's certainly challenging to risk moving into unfamiliar territory when we have no way to know if what we're doing will make a real difference.

Choosing to abandon our well ordered routines and established habit patterns in order to set off in a very different direction is all the more daunting as it means we have to risk encountering some very real psychological and maybe even physiological resistance. Psychologists call this mental malaise associated with venturing into unfamiliar circumstances, *cognitive dissonance.*[62]

In practical terms, cognitive dissonance is akin to what we experience when we are flying on a commercial jetliner and unexpectedly encounter a patch of rough air in the form of turbulence. If you've ever experienced turbulence, you'll likely agree that your first reaction is to check your safety belts; your first thoughts are that what you're experiencing is uncomfortable and, quite likely, very unsettling. Whereas a moment ago you were enjoying a smooth ride, now your expectations have been interrupted. The worse the turbulence, the more it bothers you, and the faster you want it to go away.

Much like the disruptive turbulence you encounter when you're flying, cognitive dissonance is a form of *turbulence for your brain*. It's a warning to you that things are not as they should be and, in order to restore order, you need to deal with the turbulence in some form or fashion.

And deal with it soon.

The reason this brain turbulence bothers us so much stems from our innate need for consistency in our lives. We want things to work the same every time they happen. When we awake in the morning, we want to find the floor under our feet, the sky above our heads, and nice, hot coffee in our cups. And in the same way we expect these kinds of physical consistencies, we also expect psychological consistencies. If we had a job, a spouse, and a family yesterday, we expect to find them in pretty much the same condition today. This reinforces why a mediocre me mindset, in an attempt to minimize brain turbulence, does everything possible to convince us to avoid change and keep doing things the same old way.

CAUTION

Experiencing some momentary brain discomfort…is a sure-tell sign you're moving in the right direction

But if we are more inclined to lean into change instead of surrendering our power to act when life throws us a curveball then let's be clear. Brain turbulence comes with the territory. It's a natural byproduct of stretching our potential, expanding our capacities, and growing into the kind of leader we want to be and others deserve to see.

Will it be easy?

Nope.

Will it be comfortable?

Unlikely.

But will it be worth it?

Well, that depends on how we choose to draw our lines of personal responsibility. Broad lines mean we are willing to risk experiencing some brain turbulence if doing so will help promote positive outcomes in our sphere of influence; narrow lines mean leaving the work of improving conditions in our surroundings to someone else. If we chose the former and are intent to grow into the best version of ourselves, my military advice is simple: armor up and move out. Accept that experiencing some momentary discomfort in the process of being the difference we want to see occur around us is a sure-tell sign we are moving in the right direction.

Parting Thoughts

One day, a farmer who loved nature was walking in the woods near his farm and came across an injured baby eagle that had fallen far from her nest. Knowing it would very likely die unless something was done to help her, he gathered her carefully in his hands and took her home.

The attentive nurturing and care the little eagle received from the farmer quickly restored her to health. Soon it began spending time in the barnyard with some of the farmer's other animals, particularly the chickens and turkeys. These feathered friends ate together every day, and the eagle quickly grew to full size—complete with a fifteen-foot wingspan.

Seeing the eagle was healthy and ready to leave the safety of the barnyard and set out on her own, the farmer decided it was time for the eagle to learn how to fly. So he contacted a naturalist friend of his who agreed to come and help.

One morning the two men stepped into the barnyard, and the naturalist picked up the eagle, gave her a toss into the wind, and said, "Fly!" But the eagle just sunk to the ground, rejoined her earthbound feathered friends, the turkeys and the chickens, and joined them in pecking away at their food.

The farmer and his friend repeated this same exercise many times over the course of the next two weeks, but despite their numerous attempts, they always met with the same results. The eagle had no interest in flying and was more than content to walk across the yard instead of soaring above the earth. But then the naturalist came up with an idea. "Be ready early tomorrow morning, and I will come and get you and the eagle," he said to his farmer friend.

The next day the naturalist picked up the farmer and led him and the eagle to the top of a nearby mountain, just before dawn. Above and below them eagles were flying high and low, soaring effortlessly against the backdrop of a sky, alive with the promise of a new day.

The eagle, used to being confined by the limited earthly bounds of the barnyard, was astounded by what she was seeing. However, after only a few short minutes, her astonishment gave way to curiosity, and she began to look inquisitively at the strange new sights around her. She had never seen birds, much less eagles like herself, enjoying the freedom wrought by unencumbered flight. In that moment, inspired by *the example she saw before her*, the eagle shuddered with what seemed like new life and spread her wings fully for the first time. Then she mounted the wind and began to fly, never to return to the narrow confines of the barnyard again.

To be fair, it's easy to understand why an eagle that's never flown can so easily surrender something as significant and majestic as the gift of flight. After all, it doesn't know what it's missing. It hasn't yet discovered what it feels like to be freed from earthly bounds. Nor has it ever experienced the sensation of soaring amongst the clouds, gliding along almost effortlessly, buoyed by the invisible currents of the wind.

Another thing the eagle doesn't realize is the significance her surroundings have on how she chooses to live her life. I'm not speaking solely of her physical surroundings, but primarily of her personal surroundings. Slowly, insidiously, naive to the full effect the example of her flightless feathered friends has on her life, she became content pecking about the barnyard despite possessing the potential to do so much more. Settling for a life far smaller and narrower than she's capable of achieving, she surrendered one of her greatest strengths, the ability to fly, without even putting up a fight.

Many of us forget how easy it is to become like the eagle in this story. After all, we too can be lulled into thinking our current circumstances are as good as it gets. We too can lose sight of the significant influence those we choose to surround ourselves with have on our lives. Just as we too can forget how settling for the comfort and safety of the status quo is an impediment to our growing into the best version of ourselves possible.

As the once-earthbound eagle in our story affirms, we are the primary architects of our reality. What we choose to do and who we choose to do it with makes all the difference in determining if we, in the end, will succeed in pursuing a path that will enable us to lead our lives in a more excellent way. Leaving each of us to ask ourselves if the example we are currently projecting in our proverbial "barnyards" is encouraging others to accept mediocrity or challenging them to stretch their abilities and discover the full extent of their capabilities so they too can become the best version of themselves possible?

Chapter 8

Reclaim Responsibility

Leadership, like responsibility, is a voluntary act.
—John C. Maxwell

In the spring of 1943, a B-17 bomber departed its base in England on a mission to bomb the German City of Kassel. Just weeks earlier, the Allied forces had learned that this particular location was one of the Nazi's primary ammunition producers. As the crew of this particular aircraft, *The Tondelayo*, neared their target, they found themselves barraged by heavy flak from antiaircraft guns. This was not particularly unusual for a daylight bombing mission over enemy territory, but on this occasion an enemy round hit one of the plane's internal fuel tanks. Miraculously, the twenty-millimeter incendiary shell failed to explode. Dumbfounded, Captain Bohn Fawkes and his crew were quietly thankful for this unexpected miracle.

Upon landing, the crew assessed their heavily scarred aircraft, marveling at the workmanship that enabled this flying machine to withstand such an incredible amount of damage while still maintaining its ability to fly. Summoning his crew chief, the man who would be

76

leading the repair efforts, Captain Fawkes asked for the unexploded shell that had hit the aircraft. The captain wanted to keep it as a souvenir of the crew's unbelievable luck.

The crew chief agreed, offering to bring it to the crew's debriefing room at their squadron's headquarters as soon as possible.

A little more than an hour later, the chief arrived at the briefing room, an unexploded shell in hand and a strange look on his face. Stammering at first, seemingly unsure how to start or what to say, he finally simply blurted out that he'd discovered not just one shell in the fuel tank, but eleven—eleven unexploded shells with enough potential explosive power to destroy several aircraft.

Bohn and his crew were awestruck, unsure of how something like this could occur. Something that seemingly defied all odds...until he heard the next words out of the crew chief's mouth. "Sir, the shells that hit your aircraft had no explosive charges. They were clean as a whistle and completely harmless. Empty.

"All but one, that is."

As it turns out, one of the eleven shells contained a carefully rolled piece of paper. On it, scrawled in Czech, were the words: "*This is all I can do for you now.*"[63]

Somewhere, in an armament factory behind enemy lines, someone had chosen to render the shells inert and unable to bring about the pain and destruction they were designed to deliver. The unexpected actions of at least one brave man or woman in doing what they could, when they could, where they could to positively influence conditions in their surroundings teach us a valuable lesson about leadership. That is, it is not primarily a matter of title, rank or position; *it is a matter of behavior*. It's about willingly doing something to build value into our surroundings—one opportunity at a time.

Dispelling Myths

The dictionary reminds us that leading means going ahead or showing the way. As such, when people today hear the term *leadership*, often the first thought that comes to mind is of a head of state moving their nation to action, generals leading armies into battle, or captains of industry guiding products to market.[64] From such a limited view, leaders are believed to be people in positions of authority who possess special talents or skills, or those who have been elected, appointed, trained, or ordained to lead.

The Distinguished Service Professor at Harvard University's Kennedy School of Government, Dr. Joseph Nye, once wrote how "Americans have long been ambivalent about leaders, and the problem is not limited to the Unites States. Polls show similar results in many countries." While this may make us think our current leadership crisis is nothing new, Dr. Nye goes on to add that "the context of leadership is changing," and many people today have not yet caught on.[65]

But it's certainly not for lack of trying.

One recent study of leadership counted 221 different definitions from the period of the 1920s to the 1990s alone, with the earliest definitions emphasizing the ability of a leader to *impress* his or her will on others. Later definitions emphasized more mutuality and power sharing between leaders and followers.[66] In either view, the literature largely agrees that leadership is about wielding some form of personal power to mobilize others for a purpose. Just as it confirms leaders have a profound influence on the behavior of those around them, for better or worse.

This truth was made abundantly clear to me several years ago while serving as the wing commander at Grand Forks Air Force Base in North Dakota. Given that I was accountable for several billion dollars of aircraft and infrastructure, the safe and effective accomplishment of a global military mission, and most importantly, the care of almost six-thousand people on our five-thousand-plus-acre installation, it's certainly safe to say I received a lot of attention as the unit's leader. In fact, with the title of wing commander came a special car. Termed the "White Top," its roof was literally painted white (the rest of the car was dark blue), so wherever I went, people knew the boss was present. I was also provided a designated house, more reserved parking spaces on the base than I could ever possibly use, and ample opportunities to give speeches, pin medals, present awards, and promote people to their next rank or job. And although my role as designated leader was clearly the most visible, the indispensible daily work of keeping airplanes fixed and flying, ensuring the base was secure and our people properly trained, and attending to a host of other critical factors was the work of thousands of other men and women who, operating far from the spotlight, were the true key to our organization's success. So while it was true I was the name and face at the top of the proverbial pyramid and organizational chart, I knew quite well that leadership was occurring all around me, as men and women operating at all levels and ranks, *willingly accepted responsibility* for taking the initiative to use their influence to build value into their surroundings.

Responsibility: The Key to Effective Leadership

The late, prolific US Air Force General Curtis E. LeMay was fond of saying that if he had to come up with one word to define leadership, it would be "responsibility."

He could not have been more right.

The main concept of responsibility is that we are being entrusted by a higher authority to care for something or someone—and along with this trust comes the blessings associated with doing it well or the consequences of doing it poorly.[67] To embrace responsibility means cultivating and protecting those things you are immediately accountable for in your surroundings. Be it as a parent, pastor, politician, or as the inspiring example of the unknown factory worker in world War II affirms, in any role we may fulfill.

Sociologists tell us human beings are inclined to accept responsibility most naturally and effectively when (1) it is clear to us that the primary responsibility for the well-being of others *rests on us and that others are relying on us*, and (2) when we have been trained from an early age to *recognize and assume that responsibility faithfully*. The first point speaks to our accepting responsibility when we realize others are depending on us. The second confirms we learn responsibility primarily by *observing how others lead their lives*—serving as yet another powerful reminder that what we choose to do, or not do for that matter, makes a difference; likely more so than we may have ever imagined.

What's clear in this description is that it makes no accommodation for mediocrity, nor should it. After all, mediocrity detests having to account for its own actions. It prefers to act on its own terms when it's practical, convenient, or comfortable. But as you and I both know from our own experiences, stepping up to plant the seeds of positive progress when and where we can is rarely practical, convenient, or much less comfortable. Making it easy to understand why our possessing a mediocre me mindset conditions us to avoid responsibility at each and every turn.

Think about it.

If we willingly raise our hands to own a problem, act on an opportunity, or agree to try and be part of the solution to an existing

NOTE
To embrace responsibility means cultivating and protecting those things you are immediately accountable for in your surroundings

challenge, we position ourselves to potentially experience regret, loss, or even failure. And as we'll explore a little later, we just don't naturally enjoy putting ourselves in positions that disrupt our seemingly well-ordered worlds and established routines.

The greatest challenge posed by such thinking, however, is that it leads us to conveniently forget one of history's repeated lessons. Namely, that we are at our individual and collective best not when we are sitting on the sidelines simply observing what's happening around us, but when we routinely exercise the strength of character to think differently, act boldly, and be the best version of ourselves possible by doing something to set into motion a cycle of positive change when and where we can.

No matter where we currently find ourselves in the proverbial hierarchy, organizational chart, or established social order.

Choosing to Make a Positive Difference

Kelley lives in Texas and builds custom swimming pools for a living. Well, most of the time, anyway. With the economy putting a significant dent in his business and drain on his pocketbook, he has had to moonlight recently.

Now Kelley also repossesses cars.

One morning during the 2010 Christmas season, Kelley set out to a suburb of Dallas to pick up a vehicle for a used-car client.

Normally he prefers to go late at night or in the early hours of the morning so he can avoid trouble. After all, in his words, "It's easier work if you don't get caught."

No doubt it's also probably safer, as repossessing cars can be an emotionally charged situation for those on the "business end" of the transaction.[68]

But on this particular day, Kelley didn't have that luxury, as the dealer wanted the car repossessed immediately. So he set out to retrieve the vehicle. Arriving late in the morning, he spied the car in the driveway and planned to quietly slip in and be gone before anyone noticed.

But for some reason, today was different. He chose to knock on the door of the trailer first, something in his own admission he rarely ever does.

Connie Henderson answered his knock, not expecting the repo man. But then again, she wasn't surprised either. After all, she had lost her job as an accounting clerk a month earlier. Living with her mom, Henderson had informed the car dealer she could not afford the payments until she got a job. But a deal was a deal and the car had to go. It's the way the system is designed to work.

Henderson, never having a car repossessed before, stood at the front door looking into the face of the man who was here to take her last significant earthly possession. She tried to be brave about it, knowing it was going to be a lot harder to find a job without wheels of her own. Quietly setting out to remove her personal possessions from the car, she began to share her personal situation with Kelley.

Kelley recalls being struck by how polite and kind she was to him, despite the fact he was here to take away her only means of transportation. As he was pulling out of the driveway, he remembers seeing Connie standing there, watching the vehicle drive away, large tears streaming down her face.

In that moment, although he had never felt this way before, Kelley knew he had to do something to help. Instead of simply doing his job as he had so many times before, he chose to risk deviating from his routine and *accepted responsibility for leading the change he wanted to see in his surroundings.*

Acting on this unexpected opportunity to build value into another's life, he immediately called a friend who owned a used-car lot in the city, asking him if he had a good, reliable car he could sell him—cheap. As it turns out, he did. A 1990 Chevy Lumina in excellent shape.

He agreed to sell it at cost.

Kelley then set out to call other friends, inquiring if they would help donate money to pay for the car. One friend, a banker, seeing a side of Kelley he had never experienced, was glad to contribute to the worthy cause. Within hours, Kelley raised the money and was driving to pick up the used vehicle when his cell phone rang.

It was his car dealer friend.

"I've been thinking about the situation," he said and "I'll let you have the car. Just give her the money you've collected to help with Christmas."

NOTE
Accepting responsibility for our choices actually calms our minds and clarifies our vision. It soothes our emotions and enables us to think and act more positively and constructively

Now holding back tears himself, Kelley called Henderson and broke her the news. She couldn't believe her ears.

"Never in my life did I think they were going to give me this car," she later told a reporter. "And when he handed me a check, too? Who expects that?"[69]

Although Kelley didn't know what prompted him to initially act, he is surely glad he did. For in that moment of seizing the initiative to do something to positively influence outcomes in his surroundings, he affirms we are all capable of being *a force for good in our part of the world.*

We just have to choose to get off the fence and into the game.

Ignorance Isn't an Option

According to the dictionary, *ignorance* is defined as "being uneducated, unaware, or uniformed." When we're ignorant, we don't know what we don't know. As a result, it is easy to let ourselves off the hook for what happens around us.

Insanity, on the other hand, has been described as doing or believing "the same thing over and over again and expecting different results."[70] It reveals we know better, but we choose not to change what we do or how we think. One extreme (ignorance) liberates us from the responsibility of having to make an informed choice. The other (insanity) makes us accountable for having to decide how we will think or act when facing the need to respond to circumstances occurring around us.

Though ignorance can be bliss, insanity is of our own choosing.

How does this relate to leadership, you ask?

It's simple.

We can choose to continue to possess a traditional, confining view of leadership by seeing it as something requiring a particular position, rank, role, or title. Or, we can adopt a broader view. Choosing to see leadership first and foremost as *a choice* to do what we can, when we can, where we can to try and positively influence outcomes in our spheres of influence. And although that choice is ours and ours alone, know this. When it comes to expanding our thinking about leadership, we can't continue to say we don't know any better.

Ignorance is no longer an option.

Parting Thoughts

Years ago, the Kellogg Foundation published a report on the status of leadership on university campuses across America. The study included both public and private schools and provided some very intriguing conclusions. Most notably it confirmed the following beliefs among college students:

- Everyone has the potential to be a leader.
- Leadership cannot be separated from values.
- Leadership must be actively practiced.
- In today's world, everyone needs to develop their leadership skills.[71]

What this tells us is that more and more people today believe leadership is a 360 degree proposition. Because we all wield some measure of influence, be it in our home, workplace, worship space, or community, we all have opportunities to lead. We can all lead up, we can lead across, and we can lead down. But someone has to choose to accept responsibility for taking the initiative to go first in leading the change they want to see occur in their surroundings.

When I was a squadron commander in Wichita, Kansas, a friend gave me a simple, framed quote that had been found written on the tomb of an Anglican Bishop in the crypts of Westminster Abbey in England. The words read:

> When I was young and free and my imagination had no limits, I dreamed of changing the world. As I grew older and wiser, I discovered the world would not change, so I shortened my sights and decided to change only my country.
>
> But it, too, seemed immovable. As I grew into my twilight years, in one last desperate attempt, I settled for changing only my family, those closest to me, but alas, they would have none of it.
>
> And now as I lie on my deathbed, I suddenly realize: If I had only changed myself first, then by example I would have changed my family. From their inspiration and encouragement, I would then have been able to better my country and, who knows, I may have even changed my world.

Over the last decade that I've had this quote in my possession, I can't tell you how many times I've paused to read it. And here's why. Out of all the definitions of leadership I've encountered; all the books on leadership I've read; and all the courses, programs, and seminars on leadership I've attended; the simplicity of these words perhaps captures it best. Leading is *a choice* to accept responsibility for taking the initiative to promote the change we want to see occur in our surroundings—one opportunity at a time.

Those who set their hearts and minds to leading their lives in a more excellent way understand that responsibility is a game changer. In fact, scientists and psychologists confirm that accepting responsibility for our choices actually calms our minds and clarifies our vision. It soothes our emotions and enables us to think and act more positively and constructively, providing us an enhanced sense of control over outcomes that is missing when we settle to be mere observers in the journey we call life.

The Third Choice

LOVE THY NEIGHBOR...
BE COMPASSIONATE

No act of kindness, no matter how small, is ever wasted.
—Aesop

Chapter 9

Practice Jen

*The most satisfying thing in life is to have been
able to give a large part of oneself to others.*
—**Pierre Tielhard de Chardin, French Philosopher**

The great Chinese philosopher Confucius was born into a world experiencing widespread social anarchy.[72] Rival political factions sought to gain greater control in order to consolidate power, and warring states made a regular habit of invading one another. People were slaughtered by the thousands, often simply to further one leader's personal political ambitions, leaving a wake of death, destruction, pain, and sorrow everywhere.

It was truly a dark time in Chinese history.

However, born from Confucius' first-hand experience with these atrocities was a commitment to doing what he could, when he could, where he could to reinvent the social and moral order of society; to do something that would turn back the tide of darkness that had enveloped his beloved country; to act on the belief that those who chose to cause yesterday's pain need not be allowed to control tomorrow's potential.

Acting contrary to many of the leading philosophers and rulers of his time who believed the only way to control human behavior was to dominate it, Confucius chose otherwise. Instead, he grounded his teachings around the concept of *jen*: a way of being in the world best characterized by such terms as virtue, goodness, charity, humanity, and love.[73]

This earliest Confucian view of *jen* emphasized honoring relationships. Primarily those relationships between the Emperor and his court officials; parents and their children; husbands and wives; and anyone else that held some measure of influence in the lives of those placed in their immediate care. Practicing *jen* then meant people were to always have others best interest at heart.

It was truly a selfless ideal born amidst a very selfish world.

Over the next hundred years, *jen* continued to evolve.[74] Emphasis was increasingly placed on the fact that everyone possessed innate value and any difference in wealth or societal status should not affect how people are treated. Admittedly, this was a very progressive perspective for a society that viewed their appointed leaders, the Emperors in particular, as direct descendants of the gods themselves.[75] Nonetheless, *jen* continued to gain momentum to the point that treating others with respect, dignity and genuine care and concern was to be the rule, not the exception. Especially when carrying out one's responsibilities as a leader.[76]

Although many reading this may have never previously heard of the term *jen*, there's little question you're familiar with the characteristic it represents: Love.[77] In particular, an *altruistic form of love* that is unlimited, unselfish, and affirming of others.[78] A love that always seeks another's wellbeing and reinforces the age-old truth we are at our best not when we are focusing on ourselves but rather, when we willfully submit ourselves in service to something bigger than ourselves.[79]

Re-Discovering *Jen*

Coined by the philosopher Auguste Comte, the word "altruism" derives from the Latin *alter*, or "other," and has long dominated discussions of how people can best behave towards those around them.[80] This *others-centered* orientation is at the heart of the concept of *jen* and is widely lauded as a foundation of moral life. In fact, literature from around the world tells story after story of individuals who experienced positive changes in their personality and overall sense of well-being after being exposed to the power of such a selfless form of sacrificial, self-giving love.[81]

Of course, to many this concept may sound soft and far from how they are used to thinking about leadership. But, if (arguably) the most powerful man in the world thinks there's merit to this others-centered approach to leading, then surely its worth considering.

In a speech during his first month in office, U.S. President Barack Obama shared how he too believes that one rule binds all peoples together, regardless if they are leader or led: "It is an ancient rule; a simple rule; but also one of the most challenging." He adds, "For it asks each of us to take some measure of *responsibility* for the well-being of people we may not know or worship with or agree with on every issue. Sometimes, it asks us to reconcile with bitter enemies or resolve ancient hatreds... It requires us not only to believe, but to do – to give something of ourselves for the benefit of others and the betterment of our world."[82] For some, this rule of ethical conduct is best captured in the words; 'Do unto others as you would have them do unto you,' or, in even simpler terms, 'love thy neighbor as thyself.'[83] In the Jewish tradition, it's expressed simply as 'That which is hateful to you, do not do to your fellow.'[84] In Islam, this ideal is captured in the simple phrase, 'None of you truly believes until he wishes for his brother what he wishes for himself.'[85]

As it turns out, the evolved concept of *jen*, is nothing more than what many of us across the world commonly refer to as "the Golden Rule."[86] It's a rule that, in my view, is perhaps more relevant for leaders at every level to grasp today than it's ever been. A rule that challenges us to think differently, act boldly, and strive to become the best version of ourselves possible by modeling a more excellent way to lead our lives each day in tangible ways.

The Transformative Power of Jen

Maly's Father died when she was a baby. While still a toddler, her mother became ill with tuberculosis and could no longer work. The family suddenly found themselves with no means to make ends meet, so Maly began scrounging in the local city streets.

Barely ten years old and still begging for a living Maly, came across a series of men who, instead of offering her help or hope, sexually exploited her.

Shortly thereafter, she turned to child prostitution as a way to feed her ailing mother. Her mother did not know what her daughter had to go through in order to get that plate of rice on the table every evening. And young Maly, filled with guilt and shame, never told her.

Several months after her eleventh birthday, Maly was again scrounging for food when she was assaulted by several men. Physically and mentally traumatized by the brutal attack, she was subsequently institutionalized in a government facility. In short order, however, she escaped and began roaming the streets. After several years, feeling increasingly worthless and lost, she became convinced no one could ever possibly love her again for who she really was.

As it turns out, she was mistaken.

Local workers for an organization called simply, *Love146*, men and women committed to eliminating the sexual exploitation of children across the globe, found Maly and took her in. They provided her with not only food and clothing to feed and clothe her ailing body, but shared unconditional love and acceptance to nourish her broken spirit. Today, because of the willingness of a small group of leaders to do what they could, when they could, where they could to live out the Golden Rule, Maly has been liberated from the horror and pain of sexual abuse and is experiencing love as she has never known it before.[87]

Increasing our Capacity for Good

Think about the simplicity of the Golden Rule: "Do Unto others as you would have them do unto you." Or, said even more succinctly, *"Love thy neighbor."*

That's it.

Three words packed with enough power to positively influence every element of our lives. Be it our marriage, our family relationships, work relationships or friendships, putting the golden rule of *jen* into practice day in and day has the potential to transform even the most heartbreaking predicaments into hope-filled outcomes.[88]

And I can prove it.

Years ago, Dr. Karl Menninger, a renowned doctor and psychologist at a psychiatric hospital, was seeking the cause of many of his patient's ills. One day he decided to call in his staff and proceeded to unfold a plan for developing in his clinic an atmosphere reflecting the Golden Rule. He directed all patients be given large quantities of unconditional love. No unloving attitudes were to be displayed in the presence of patients. Doctors and nurses were challenged to go about their work with a commitment to treating their neighbor (or in this case, their patient) as they themselves would like to be treated if the roles were reversed.

At the end of six months, the time spent by patients in the institution was cut in half![89]

Psychologist, sociologist, and theologians tell us *jen* works because it is designed to nurture positive interactions that build value into others. These interactions, which grow out of a belief in the highest ideal of human nature, provide a host of benefits. Serving as a source of enrichment and vitality for ourselves and those around us;[90] equipping us to adapt and bounce back from difficult circumstances; and, empowering us to seek new levels of creativity, trust and cooperation.[91]

Thus, as Dr. Menninger's experience reminds us, when we make it a priority to first practice *jen* with all those we encounter, we enhance everyone's capacity for good—yet another reminder of how the most effective leaders in our lives are those who are willing to do something to bring out the best in us—one opportunity at a time.

Small Actions, Big Outcomes

The Oscar-winning film *The Blind Side* recounts the story of the Tuohy family and their adopted son, professional football player Michael Oher. Their story of extraordinary generosity captured the hearts and imaginations across the globe. If you watched the movie or read the book, you'll recall how a wealthy, white family tried to help an underprivileged black teen, eventually adopting him as their son and changing his life forever. It powerfully illustrates how choosing to make a positive difference in others' lives most often starts with a single, small action. What may be lost on both the reader and the viewer, however, is that the Tuohys' decision to help this young man in his moment of need did not occur in an instant, but rather reflected a commitment to leading their lives in a more excellent way developed over the course of a lifetime.

In their latest book, *In a Heartbeat*, the Tuohys share how people who so badly want to model a better way to be in the world often wait for a particular cause to come along, or until conditions are just right. "When I retire, I'll donate more of my time and talent to charity." "When my bonus check arrives, I'll give a little more to a worthwhile cause."[92] But such an approach reflects a somewhat rigid, and to be honest, measured approach to giving. It reveals we may inadvertently be caught up in pursuing particular procedures and methods of giving, rather than focusing on the simplest kind of giving. The kind that flows from a sincere desire to *love your neighbor as you love yourself.*

As the Tuohys' selfless example reminds us, acting on opportunities to build value into our surroundings isn't about waiting for a particular compelling cause to come along. Instead, it's choosing to act on behalf of the person standing right in front of you. The elderly woman you almost looked right past in the grocery store taking things out of her basket because she was short on cash; the disabled veteran at the corner, looking for his next meal; or the single mother you sit next to in church who doesn't know how she'll make ends meet for her and her children this month.

> **NOTE**
>
> *Making a positive difference in the world…results from a commitment to serving our neighbor by choosing to do small things with great love*

Ultimately, putting *Jen* into practice wherever we choose to lead is to embrace the realization that it's not the size of our gifts that matter, but our willingness to reject mediocrity and deviate from the comfort of our routines to do what we can, when we can, where we can for those who need our help the most. Then, perhaps we too will learn the same lesson the Tuohys did. Namely, how making a positive difference in the world rarely occurs by a carrying out a single great act, but instead results from a commitment to serving our neighbor by choosing to do small things with great love—one opportunity at a time.

Parting Thoughts

During one of the Turkish persecutions of the Armenians, a young girl and her brother were pursued by a bloodthirsty Turkish soldier. He trapped them at the end of the lane and killed the brother before the sister's eyes. She managed to escape by leaping over the wall and fleeing into the countryside. Years later, now serving as a nurse, a wounded soldier was brought into her hospital. She recognized him at once as the soldier who had killed her brother and had tried to kill her. His condition was such that the least neglect or carelessness on her part would cost him his life. But instead of seeing this as an opportunity for revenge, she saw it as an opportunity to be redemptive. Giving him the most painstaking and constant care possible.

Weeks passed and the soldier, now well on the road to recovery, recognized the nurse as the girl whose brother he had slain. "Why have you done this for me who killed your brother?" he asked. Her answer was simple, but profoundly powerful: "because I believe there is greater power in loving thy neighbor than there is in hating thy enemy."[93]

Today, those of us committed to being part of the solution to our society's most pressing problems must choose to make this evolved concept of *jen* real in our homes, workplaces, worship spaces, and communities. Be it with siblings, parents, children, husbands, wives, workmates, or classmates, when we choose to do our part to model the same compassion, kindness, and respect we ourselves desire, then learning to treat others as we ourselves would like to be treated no longer seems so difficult.

Jen then serves as a tangible expression of our commitment to think more broadly about our potential role in the world. It reminds us that love is the antidote for conflict, anger, hatred and fighting between people, and ultimately, even between societies and nations. Perhaps this is why love has been called the crowning grace of humanity, the light of the soul, and the golden link which binds us all together. It reflects a way of thinking and being that motivates us to say no to the status quo and yes to accepting responsibility for leading the change we want to see occur in our surroundings.

One cannot help but wonder how things might be different around us if love routinely expressed itself in ways that brought out the best in everyone? In the words of Rob Morris, President and co-founder of Love 146, creating such a world will not happen by accident. It must be intentional. "That sort of change," he says, "often starts with one voice, but when one voice gets added to another voice, and added to another voice, it becomes this great collective shout. That shout leads to action and that's when change happens."

Chapter 10

Suffer With Affection

Love and compassion are necessities, not luxuries.
Without them humanity cannot survive.
—Dalai Lama

In December 2006, Marine Colonel (now Major General), Juan Ayala was serving as the senior advisor to the 1ˢᵗ Iraqi Army Division headquartered in Habbaniyah, Iraq. In this key role, General Ayala advised, trained, and mentored the Iraqi Army in order to prepare them for the eventual task of securing and defending their own country from radical extremists.

It was a role requiring patience, resolve and as it turns out, compassion.

One evening, about midnight, an Iraqi private knocked on the door of Ayala's room. He was surprised, not because of the late hour, but by the fact that the Iraqi was a private—and he was a Colonel—and the Iraqis are very rank conscious. The man standing before him appeared to be in his fifties and had clearly been crying. The Iraqi soldier immediately got to the point. "You saw my son die today: I want you to send me to him so I can take him home—you understand as a father."[94]

Earlier in the day, a combat outpost had been attacked while Colonel Ayala and the Iraq Commanding General were visiting. Numerous casualties were rushed to a medical facility. While there, a number of Iraqi's nervously paced as they waited to find out the status of their comrades. One of the soldiers was clearly beyond help. Shrapnel had claimed his life.

As the American Marine Colonel faced the grieving Iraqi private in front of him, it dawned on him that both father and Son had been serving in the same unit and had been together on this fateful patrol. The father had witnessed a parent's greatest nightmare, the death of their child. And it was quite likely there were others sons and relatives on the same patrol, as well.

Desperate to see his son one final time and committed to granting him a proper funeral; the Iraqi father had come to the American officer for help. The Iraqi leadership had already told him they could do nothing to assist. It was beyond their control.

Overcome by compassion for this grieving father and fellow warrior and, despite the lack of an established chain of protocol to address such an event, the U.S. Marine Colonel secured transportation and delivered the Iraqi soldier to his fallen son for a final goodbye—revealing himself in that moment to be a leader who understood that compassion is not a tool of the weak, but rather, a commitment made by those who are strong. Specifically, it's a commitment to do something, big or small, to transform the desire to build value into others lives into tangible action—one opportunity at a time.

Compassion: Love in Action

The Dalai Lama is known for his many wise and insightful sayings. One of his favorites, by his own admission, is "if you want *others* to be happy, practice compassion."[95] He then is quick to add that "If *you* want to be happy, practice compassion." What this famous Buddhist leader is speaking to is the timeless truth that in life, we just can never give or get too much compassion.

Admittedly, this is exactly the kind of advice you would expect from a widely-known religious leader like the Dalai Lama. However, what few realize is the concept of compassion extends well beyond

the bounds of theological
and philosophical tradition
and is now influencing a
host of scientific fields such
as neurology, endocrinology
and even immunology. All of

NOTE
*Compassion is...to
suffer with affection
for another*

which are proving the profoundly positive physical and psychological benefits of regularly setting aside our own agendas and choosing to love thy neighbor by doing something to practice compassion in our interactions with others.

As the story of General Ayala reveals, compassion can be a very powerful force for good. Operating much like its close cousin, empathy, it opens us up to feeling others suffering so we can make ourselves useful to them in their moment of need. Perhaps it should not be surprising to us that the word compassion derives from the Latin root *com* and *passio* as well as the Greek word *patheia*. Taken together, this literally translates as "[to] suffer with affection."

From such a view, compassion reflects a willingness to think of ourselves less and willingly enter into a person's situation in their moment of brokenness, heartache and hurt.[96] It communicates to others by our words and our ways that their welfare and well-being is important to us. So much so, in fact, that we are intent to slow down our lives long enough to ensure they know that "I *see* you in your moment of hardship and I'm here if you need me."

I'll never forget learning how important this concept of people feeling "seen" really is, especially during those periods of life when things are most difficult and daunting.

Years ago, while in Seattle completing my post-graduate work, I was privileged to work with a number of homeless youth. Of course, given the many reasons young people turn to the streets is well researched and documented, those I spent time with over the months were certainly no exception. However, my purpose was not to explore the *why* they were on the street but *what* it is these young people wanted most out of life.[97] The ultimate goal of my research being to better understand the motivational factors that can be utilized to help those facing particularly challenging circumstances to consider setting aside the fears they possess in the

NOTE
*Feeling valued by
others is fundamental
to our happiness
and well being*

present so they can begin making different, more empowering choices in the future.

Over the course of several months, I interviewed dozens of youths ranging in age from thirteen to thirty. Meeting in groups of four to five over a cup of coffee at a local Starbucks or, in time as I became a trusted outsider, sharing a "forty" in one of their favorite alleys, I got to hear their stories first-hand. After scores of interviews, in which I would simply ask if they could have (or experience) one particular thing in this stage of their lives, what would it be? A single, primary theme emerged loud and clear as the dominant desire of their hearts.

It wasn't money.

It wasn't the desire to return home (or to even have a home, for that matter).

Nor was it a desire to be in a relationship (although I found it fascinating that these young people on the street actually self-organize into family units of sorts, but that's a different story).

It was simply that they wanted to "be seen" by those around them. Quite sadly, they relayed time-and-time again the greatest heartbreak they registered came from people passing by on the street and treating them as if they were "invisible." Be it diverting their gaze so they would not have to make eye contact, "looking past" them as if they didn't exist, or, in some cases, even choosing to cross the street rather than have to walk past them on the sidewalk.

The desire to be acknowledged as a person of innate value and worth—to be genuinely "seen" by others—was cited by well over 90% of the people I interviewed as what they desired the most.

But there's a twist to my research project I haven't told you. You see, I wasn't just conducting this study with those living on the streets. Over the same year I conducted similar discussion groups with students at a prominent public university on the East Coast and even young men and women attending one of our nation's service academies. Though their circumstances were certainly different, their responses were not. During our numerous discussions, they also ranked the desire to be seen as someone of innate significance and worth as the highest of several factors they could choose. Although some may challenge the statistical significance of these findings, or even question the size and scope of the survey groups themselves, no one can argue with the fact that what these young people were affirming is true for all of us. In short, feeling valued by others is fundamental to our happiness and well-being. It provides us with the increased sense of inner confidence we need to suspend our fears so we can continue forward in our journey to stretch and grow into the best version of ourselves possible.

People at Their Best

Research confirms that part of the unique nature of humans is that we are predisposed to look beyond how we are living in the present to how we might live in the future.[98] As far back as the age of great Greek philosophers such as Aristotle, Plato or Seneca, we keep coming back to the question, "What is the good life?" As bestselling author and social activist Jim Wallis states in his book, *Rediscovering Values*, "We seek answers not just about how the world is, but how the world should be."[99]

Cognitive scientists tell us the reason human beings are naturally drawn to the uplifting and inspiring elements of life is that we, by biological design, possess a collective propensity to be gracious and good.[100] This realization helps us to understand how rejecting mediocrity and acting on opportunities to exercise compassion in the world around us is not just a human impulse, it is actually our essence.[101]

I recall a segment from the *Today* show years ago that brought this truth to light for me. The host, Katie Couric, was interviewing a young man named Brian Bennett who had grown up in a troubled and abusive environment. He had struggled in school and had been picked on regularly at a young age. However, Brian turned his life around despite his negative circumstances and was now a successful and well-adjusted adult. When Couric asked him, "What made the difference?" the young man responded without hesitating: "The defining moment in my life occurred when a grade school teacher reminded me that I had tremendous value by telling me she cared about me and believed in me." This one person's willingness to acknowledge Brian's innate worth and value left an indelible mark on him. So much so that it encouraged

Brian to turn his life around and strive to emulate that same positive orientation with others in the future.

As the above story and my own experience working with people confirms, conducting ourselves compassionately, be it by sharing an encouraging word, lending a listening ear, or exercising a well-timed gentle touch, can change everything. It changes the way we see the world, the way we see others, and perhaps most importantly, as the story of Brian Bennett drives home, it can even change the way we see ourselves.

Got Soup?

Compassion is putting ourselves second and others first. It is rejecting selfishness and embracing service. It is realizing that our words and action can have a profoundly positive impact on those around us.

In an insightful article titled *Leading in Times of Trauma*, scientists and students from the University of Michigan and the University of British Colombia's CompassionLab report that although the leadership literature is soundly lacking in helping people understand the many individual and organizational benefits of expressing compassion, the data is overwhelming as to its profoundly positive effects.[102] These include reduced stress levels, an enhanced sense of satisfaction, higher profitability, productivity and quality, as well as increased employee retention rates.[103]

During traumatic situations, the positive effects of expressing compassion are even more compelling. Study after study has demonstrated how doing what we can, when we can, where we can to practice compassion in our surroundings benefits everyone by enhancing our capacity to heal, to learn, to adapt, and to excel both during life's good times and tough times.

One of the more inspiring stories I've come across of just how powerful a single compassionate act can really be involves a young man, his dying grandmother, and a bowl of clam chowder from Panera Bread Company. The story goes something like this: Brandon Cook, from Wilton, New Hampshire, was visiting

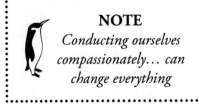

NOTE
Conducting ourselves compassionately... can change everything

his grandmother in the hospital. Terribly ill with cancer, she complained to her grandson that she loves soup and the hospital's soup was, well, inedible. If only she could get a bowl of her favorite clam chowder from Panera Bread. The challenge was, Panera only sells clam chowder on Friday and this was Tuesday. But Brandon knew this was important to her and he had to try, so he called the nearby Panera and talked to store manager Suzanne Fortier.

What happened next literally brought tears to Brandon's eyes.

Expecting to hear all the reasons why fulfilling this most unlikely of requests were too difficult, or somehow violated company policy, the store manager did just the opposite! Not only did she agree to deviate from their established schedule to make clam chowder for Brandon's ailing grandmother, she included a box of cookies and a handwritten get-well note signed by the entire staff.

It was a small act of compassion that would not normally make headlines. Except that Brandon was so moved by Suzanne's willingness to do what was right instead of what was easy, predictable, or routine, that he posted the story on his Facebook page and told his mother, Gail. Gail Cook retold the story on Panera's fan page and the rest is literally history as the post generated 500,000 (and counting) "likes" and more than 22,000 comments from customers moved by this one simple act of compassion. This single, intentional act of kindness reminding each of us to never underestimate the power a single selfless gesture can have on building value into our surroundings.

Parting Thoughts

The human experience is based on exchange and connectedness. We flourish and thrive not in isolation, but in relationship with others. This is one of the reasons suffering with affection is so powerful. Expressing compassion, whether it's by sharing a kind word, going out of our way to prepare a special meal for a sick friend or relative, or lending a helping hand, makes us feel connected and part of a group. Without compassion we are bound to feel alone, especially during those times we need others help the most.

This reminds me of the story of a frail and quite elderly man who went to live with his son, daughter-in-law, and four-year-old grandson.

The years had worked their wear upon him and the old man's hands frequently trembled, his eyesight was blurred, and his step faltered.

The family, in a gesture of togetherness, ate their meals at a common table. The elderly grandfather's shaky hands, poor muscle control and failing sight, however, made eating difficult. Peas routinely rolled off his spoon onto the floor. He often ate with his mouth open. And when he grasped his glass, milk spilled on the tablecloth. Over time, the son and daughter-in-law became irritated with the mess he made at each meal.

"We have to do something about Grandfather," the son said. "I've had enough of his spilled milk, noisy eating, and food spread all over the floor."

So the husband and wife set up a small table in the corner. There Grandfather ate alone while the rest of the family took their meal at their large dining table in the center of the room. Since in his frailty he had broken a dish or two, they also began to serve his food in a single wooden bowl.

Occasionally, when the family glanced in Grandfather's direction, they saw tears welling up in his eyes as he sat alone at his little table. The only words the couple had for him were sharp admonitions when he dropped a fork or spilled his food.

The four-year-old grandson just watched all of this in silence.

One evening before supper, the father noticed his son playing with wood scraps on the floor. He asked the child sweetly, "What are you making, my son?" Just as sweetly, the boy responded, "Oh, I am making a little bowl for you and Mama to eat your food in when I grow up." The four-year-old smiled and went back to work.

The words so struck the parents that they were speechless. Then, in a great release, tears started to stream down both their cheeks. Though no word was spoken, they both knew what had to be done. That evening the husband took Grandfather's hand and gently led him back to the family table. For the remainder of his days he ate every meal with the family . . . and, for some reason,

WARNING

Without compassion we are bound to feel alone, especially during those times we need others help the most

neither husband or wife seemed to care when a fork was dropped, milk was spilled or if the tablecloth was soiled.[104]

As the parents in the above story discovered, sometimes we must be reminded about the importance of always acting compassionately toward others. Other times, as we see in the examples of General Ayala or Panera Bread Manager Suzanne Fortier, it is a natural act of social awareness that compels us to set aside our own comfortable routines or desired agendas and enter into a person's situation in their moment of brokenness and need. And although it's unrealistic to think you can somehow eliminate all the sources of fear or suffering in others lives, you should never underestimate your ability to use your personal influence to help set into motion the healing process. For in making it a priority to communicate in tangible terms that "I see you in your moment of hardship and I'm here if you need me," you affirm you understand compassion is not about showing weakness. Nor is it soft or touchy feely. Rather, it is a tangible act of others-centered love that requires great inner strength, courage, and humility. It is one of the greatest gifts a human can bestow upon another and it is available for the taking free of charge.

Leaving each of us to ask ourselves, *what are we waiting for?*

The Fourth Choice

FIGHT FOR WHAT'S RIGHT...
BE TRUTHFUL

*Courage is not the absence of fear, but rather the
judgment that something else is more important.*
—Ambrose Redmoon

Chapter 11

Be Willing to Give It All

A tale from the Far East tells of a mouse that was so terrified of cats he would rarely risk stepping out into the world.

One day, a local magician agreed to transform the terrified mouse into a cat. This curtailed his fear and the mouse-turned-cat was happy.

That is, until he met a dog.

Now terrified of dogs, the mouse-turned-cat rarely refused to step out into the world. Yet again, the magician agreed to turn him into what he feared most—a dog.

With his latest fear now gone, the mouse-turned-cat-turned-dog was happy.

That is, until he met a lion.

So, once more, the magician agreed to turn the mouse into what he now feared the most—a lion.

Not a week later, the mouse-turned-cat-turned-dog-turned-lion came complaining to the magician that he had met a hunter and was once again afraid. However, this time the magician refused to help him, saying: "I will make you a mouse once again, for though you have the body of a lion, you still have the heart of a mouse."[105]

Does this tale sound familiar to you? Who might you know that has built a formidable exterior in order to hide a fearful interior? Have you come across any leaders in your career that found it hard not only to *make* tough decisions, but to step up and *own* those decisions? How many leaders have you known who've had the *roar* of a lion in public but the *heart* of a mouse in private?

Sadly, I think all of us have encountered people along the way whose fears and insecurities kept them from being the leaders they were capable of becoming—leaders who lacked the courage to match their proverbial "talk" to the reality of their "walk." Men and women who, like the mouse in our story, are content with coming up with countless excuses not to act when doing so is unsettling, uncomfortable, or just plain risky.

The Courage to Act

From the first days mankind began recording its history, young people have gone to war, sailors have set out to sea, and pioneers have trekked across vast tracts of wilderness to pursue new opportunities, to test their mettle, and to stretch their potential. Yet despite these clear and common examples of courage in our history books, too little modern literature addresses this topic today.

It, however, has not always been this way.

Over 2,500 years ago, Chinese philosopher Mencius said that courage is an ideal that should fuel all people's desire and ability to live a life of purpose and meaning.[106] Plato and Socrates considered courage to be not only one of the four cardinal virtues essential to leading a life of unmatched character, but also the grand virtue that made living an honorable life possible.[107]

NOTE

Courage is an ideal that should fuel all people's desire and ability to live a life of purpose and meaning

Generally, when we think of courage, the words *bravery* or *valor* come to mind. And for good reason, as these words describe the type of courage that's easiest for us to see—frequently portrayed on the nightly news in stories of soldiers selflessly serving their country in harm's way in such places as Afghanistan and Iraq, or of firemen risking their own well-being to save the life of a total stranger, or of a police officer apprehending a dangerous felon who means harm to others. This type of visible courage then reflects *the willingness to act despite the potentially paralyzing fear of injury or death.* In other words, it provides us with the *physical fortitude* to fight for what's right, no matter the potential cost to self.

Marine Corps Sergeant Rafael Peralta certainly understood and, more importantly, selflessly exemplified this type of courage.

On November 15, 2004, Sergeant Peralta and his unit were on patrol in Fallujah, Iraq. This was the seventh straight day of going house-to-house to cleanse the town of terrorists. On that particular morning, the patrol entered a home suspected of housing insurgents. Though Peralta was not assigned to enter the buildings, he chose to do so anyway.

After finding two rooms empty on the ground floor, Peralta opened a third door and was instantly hit multiple times with AK-47 fire, leaving him severely wounded. As he dropped to the floor, he moved aside in order to allow the marines behind him to return fire.

The insurgents responded by throwing a grenade at the marines. The two marines with Sgt. Peralta tried to get out of the room but could not. Sergeant Peralta, barely conscious on the floor and bleeding profusely, was able to reach for the grenade and pull it under his body absorbing the majority of the lethal blast. The shrapnel killed him instantly, but his courageous act saved the lives of his fellow marines.[108]

Sergeant Peralta was awarded the Navy Cross for his actions, the second highest military award a marine can earn. In February 2012, the Secretary of the Navy announced that one of the Navy's newest class guided-missile carriers would be named the USS *Rafael Peralta* in honor of the brave young man from San Diego.[109]

The Courage of Your Convictions

Few of us will ever find ourselves in a situation such as Sgt. Peralta's. One in which we will have to choose to give our lives to save others from imminent harm or even death. But each and every day we do encounter opportunities to exercise a different form of courage. Philosophers, theologians, and ethicists like to term this the courage of our convictions or, more commonly, *moral courage.*

Moral courage, in the words of Rushworth Kidder and Martha Bracy of the Institute for Global Ethics, is "the quality of mind and spirit that enables someone to face ethical dilemmas and moral wrongdoings firmly and confidently, without flinching or retreating."[110] Unlike physical courage, which can be displayed equally by those who strive to live honorably and those who do not, moral courage is only exemplified by those who possess the *internal strength of character* to do what's right, no matter the potential cost to self.

I learned the important distinction between these two types of courage many years ago in the course of my first flying assignment after pilot training. I was assigned to Langley Air Force Base in Hampton, Virginia to fly the C-21, which is the military version of the Lear 35. A small, sleek, fast corporate jet, the C-21 is used to move VIPs throughout the United States, South America, and Canada.

It was truly an incredible experience.

Shortly after learning how to fly the aircraft, I remember being given a book to read about the legendary creator of the Learjet, Bill Lear. Lear, it turns out, was many things: an inventor, aviator, and business leader who held more than one hundred fifty patents in electronics and aerodynamics.[111] These inventions included the eight-track stereo tape player, various altitude and directional gyros for aircraft autopilots, the first lightweight affordable radio compass, as well as a new form of a battery for car radios.[112] He was a brilliant, creative man who was always pushing the envelope of science and technology.

In the 1950s, with corporations across the nation rapidly expanding, he sensed the need and potential for a small corporate jet. So he set pencil to paper and, building on an existing blueprint for a Swiss fighter aircraft, started to work to turn his dream into reality. In 1963, the first Learjet made its maiden voyage. A year later, Lear personally delivered his first jet to a client.[113]

The Learjet was an instant, overwhelming success, and Bill Lear immediately sold many more aircraft.

However, within the first year of production in his now bustling Learjet factory in Wichita, Kansas, Bill Lear learned that two of his jets crashed under mysterious circumstances.

The news devastated him.

No Regrets

At that particular time, fifty-five Learjets were privately owned, and Lear immediately sent word to all the owners to ground their planes until he could determine what caused the crashes. The thought that more lives might be lost was far more important to him than any adverse publicity or reduction in business orders. As he researched the ill-fated flights, Lear found what he believed to be the culprit, a simple servo that controlled several of the aircrafts' wing flight surfaces. Unable to verify the technical problem on the ground, he did not hesitate to do the only thing he could to confirm his assumption. Recreate the problem—in the air.

This was, of course, a very dangerous proposal, but that's what Bill Lear chose to do—personally. Armed with nothing but a writing pad and his notes, Lear took off to reenact the profiles of the ill-fated flights. As it turns out, he too nearly lost control and almost met the same fate as the previous two pilots. Fortunately, he managed to make it through the full round of tests and was able to verify the defect. Upon landing, Lear immediately set out to develop a new part to correct the problem. Ultimately, he refitted the entire fleet of airplanes at his own expense.[114]

Think about the moral courage it took for Bill Lear to follow that course of action. Choosing to ground the planes cost him a lot of money. Perhaps more importantly, it planted seeds of doubt in the minds of future customers. Yet his memoirs make it clear he never regretted his decision. He was a leader who was willing to risk everything—his success, his

WARNING
Moral courage is only exemplified by those who possess the internal strength of character to do what's right, no matter the potential cost to self

fortune, and even his life—to solve the mystery of those crashes, simply because he knew doing so was the right thing to do.

Our Natural Aversion to Loss

Leaders like Bill Lear inspire us. Their willingness to take a stand against injustice or push the boundaries of progress reveal firsthand how fighting for what's right is a fundamental ingredient to becoming the kind of leader we desire to be and others deserve to see. But this ideal is, of course, easier said than done. After all, one of our greatest hindrances to our abandoning mediocrity and embracing excellence as our preferred way of walking in the world is our natural *aversion to experiencing loss.*

Ori and Rom Brafman, in their book *Sway: The Irresistible Pull of Irrational Behavior,* point out that "for no apparent logical reason, we overreact to perceived loss."[115] This can apply to loss of time, loss of prestige, loss of position, loss of relationships—and the list goes on. Neuroscientists are quick to add that losing something you already have is an extremely strong motivator to stick with the status quo. It saps our strength, *steals our courage,* and deters us from making moves in new, unproven, or uncomfortable directions. But perhaps the most troubling element of our built-in desire to avoid experiencing loss is how it can set us up to make decisions that are contrary to our values.

Take the story of Captain Jacob van Zanten, once a well-established and respected airline pilot who headed the safety program at the Dutch airline, KLM—the airline who touted themselves as "the people who make punctuality possible."

In the spring of 1977, on a flight from Amsterdam to the Canary Islands, van Zanten learned that a terrorist bomb had exploded at the Las Palmas airport, where he was supposed to land. He, and scores of other flights that day, were diverted to a smaller airport 50 miles away.

After safely landing the plane, van Zanten began worrying about a number of problems that would result if he failed to take off soon. For example, the Dutch government had recently instituted a mandated rest period between flights for pilots. Anyone who violated this period could be imprisoned. This meant if he didn't depart quickly, the flight would be delayed for many more hours. Additionally, the Captain was acutely aware that staying overnight at this unexpected stop meant putting the passengers up in a hotel, which would be very costly for the airline. And if that were not enough, the rapidly deteriorating local weather was expected get far worse, further complicating an already challenging situation and perhaps even further delaying his subsequent departure.

With the prospects of waiting much longer meant losing time, money, and his long-standing reputation for punctuality. You see, the good Captain had an unrivaled, almost legendary record for on-time performance. It was a record he was, understandably, very proud of.

Ultimately, van Zanten chose to go against his better judgment and decided to take off in a thick fog—despite knowing the risks, and not receiving an appropriate

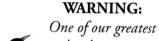

WARNING:
One of our greatest hindrances to becoming a courageous leader... is our natural aversion to experiencing loss

take off clearance—because it seemed like a now-or-never moment. Unfortunately, he didn't see the Pan Am 747 crossing the runway in front of him until it was too late—and 584 people died as a result.

The pressures and potential consequences of lost time piled up, and van Zanten fear of experiencing loss cost him, and scores of others who trusted him to do the right thing in the moment, dearly.

Overcoming Fear of Loss

Though the proceeding story of the Canary Islands tragedy is an extreme case of how fear of experiencing loss can cause someone to override their better judgment, it does serve to remind us how in everyday life we too are prone to make unintentional decisions just to avoid losing. For example, have you found yourself buying something you don't need because the deal is too good to pass up? Maybe you've stayed in a relationship you know is unhealthy and unproductive. Or, perhaps you've failed to invest in yourself, even though you're aching to expand your business but just don't want to put in the time or part with the money required to get started. Regardless of the reason, we all can likely relate to experiences in which our fear of loss led us to act in irrational ways.

This very human aversion to experiencing loss was first introduced to the world by Nobel Laureates and decision-making experts Daniel Kahneman and the late Amos Tversky. Together they postulated that the discomfort wrought by stretching outside our comfort zones is so significant that we are actually *two-and-a-half times* more prone to not act, if we perceive acting may involve a sense of loss.[116] The problem, as you can very likely surmise, is that if we can't muster the courage to move past our fear of facing loss, we cannot effectively lead. So how can we get over this mental barrier?

It turns out the key to conquering loss aversion is to become more familiar with *the cons of inaction* than it is to try and convince ourselves why we should take action. And the most effective way to assess the value of moving in a different direction is to get in the habit of asking ourselves some honest, thought-provoking questions Such as:

What am I Scared of Losing? This may seem a simple question, but we often go through life making choices without fully understanding the real motivation for doing what we are doing. By getting into the habit of taking a moment to genuinely reflect on what we fear we might lose by deciding to act, we help guard ourselves from making short-sighted choices which may result in our leading lives far smaller and narrower than we are capable of living.

What is postponing action costing me financially, emotionally and physically? Bringing to light what opportunities we will forgo or what it will tangibly cost us to stick with the status quo is proven to be one of the most effective ways to get us to risk moving in a new direction. This process of assessing the impact of a missed opportunity challenges us to explore if our rationale for not acting is primarily the result of trying to rationalize away the need for change. And without change in our lives, there is no way we can grow into the best version of ourselves. Bringing to light the age-old truth that often in life, we have to be willing to risk losing something before we can expect to gain something even better.

So What? Once we accept the reality that experiencing loss from time-to-time is inevitable if we are to stretch our abilities and explore the range of our capabilities, it's amazing how much easier it becomes to risk walking differently in the world. In fact, I've repeatedly found that the secret to routinely exercising the courage to be honest with myself about what is holding me back from doing what I know in my heart to be right in the moment, is the willingness to adopt a broader perspective of the situation. By consistently challenging myself to focus equally on all that could go right instead of just fixating on everything that might go wrong, I find myself better equipped to accept responsibility for taking the initiative to lead the change I want to see occur around me.

Understandably, our fear of loss may make it look reasonable to avoid taking gambles in life. However, the fact of the matter is, if we are willing to take the broader view and consciously bring to light both the costs of action and inaction, we will better position ourselves to experience fewer regrets and lead a life of increased meaning, significance and excellence— one opportunity at a time.

Parting Thoughts

Legend has it that during the Nazi occupation of Denmark, King Christian X noticed a Nazi flag flying over a Danish public building. He immediately called the German commandant, demanding the flag be taken down at once. The commandant refused.

"Then a soldier will go and take it down," responded the king.

"He will be shot," threatened the Nazi commandant.

"I think not," replied the king. "For I shall be that soldier."

Within minutes, the flag was taken down.

Leadership requires courage: the courage to confront reality and make tough choices; to lead change in the face of resistance; to tell the truth when it's inconvenient; to stand up for principle above expediency.

So the next time you are inclined to think:

"I don't have what it takes…"

"There is someone else better for the job…"

"If they really knew how scared I was…"

"I don't have anything valuable to contribute to the effort at hand…"

Pause to remind yourself that the true measure of leadership isn't about having all the solutions or skills required to set off in a new direction. Rather, it's choosing to transcend your fear and exercise the courage to think differently, act boldly, and be the best version of yourself even when the path is uncertain, uncomfortable, or unproven.

Sergeant Rafael Peralta was twenty-five years old when he willfully gave his life to save his fellow marines. A Mexican immigrant who enlisted the very day he received his green card, he courageously volunteered to serve on the front lines in Iraq. His bedroom at home contained three things on the walls the day he died in Iraq: a copy of the Constitution, the Bill of Rights, and Peralta's certificate of graduation from marine boot camp. Together, these items serve as visual reminders of a leader

CAUTION
*Leadership is not
a safe haven*

who understood that courage demands we be willing to take a stand for what we believe is worth fighting for in our lives when the chips are down and hard things need to get done. Leaving each of us to ask ourselves if we are ready to exercise the physical and moral courage to stand up for what we believe is good and just, important and true, no matter the potential cost to self?

Will honestly answering yes to these questions be hard?

Yup.

Will it be worth it?

I think so.

But don't just take my word for it. Ask those around you what they'd prefer: a leader with the body of a lion and the heart of a mouse, or a leader with the moral and physical courage to give their very best when anything less just won't do?

Chapter 12

Live Your Truth

*Have the courage to say no. Have the courage to face
the truth. Do the right thing because it is right. These
are the magic keys to living your life with integrity.*
—W. Clement Stone

To this day I can vividly remember the headline in the local *Stars and Stripes* newspaper in Sembach, Germany, where I grew up as a military dependent: "Over 900 Dead in Jonestown Mass Suicide." Although I was only fourteen at the time, I've never forgotten this event.

It was just that shocking.

This tragedy was the single greatest loss of American civilian life in the twentieth century.[117] At the urging of their leader, the Reverend Jim Jones, almost one thousand people willingly committing suicide. Scores of individuals, parents, grandparents, children, husbands, and wives all chose to take their own lives. Why? Here's the shocking part—they did it because they were told to do so.

For many of us, our initial response is to assume these people were just plain crazy. After all, it is certainly more frightening to consider the possibility that they were not. That these acts were driven not by mass insanity, but rather by some natural human reaction to those who exert some form of authority and power over us.

The sad truth is that the Jonestown Massacre is much more than just a stunning example of a leader whose selfish, destructive quest for control led to the death of scores of followers. It actually demonstrates how the powerful forces of unchecked obedience and unquestioned conformity can play out to their worst possible conclusion. Even more frightening, it reveals how ordinary people can be influenced to override their own better judgment and personal values without even putting up a fight.

Sometimes, as this tragedy confirms, even right to the bitter end.

Created to Belong

Conformity is a key determinant of behavior. It serves as the psychological mechanism we use to bind ourselves to systems of authority and helps us comply with expected and accepted social norms. Conforming to others' expectations is a natural and often unconscious response to fulfilling our innate desire to belong, to be part of the group, to fit in.

> **WARNING**
> *When the pressure to conform to what others are expecting or demanding of us begins to supplant our own sense of what's right and wrong… watch out*

Now this makes sense, as human beings are social creatures, and as such we are not well equipped to survive in the world alone. So we band together in different ways, calling our groups by such names as tribes, families, organizations, or a host of other descriptors that denote we are part of something larger than ourselves. This satisfies the basic needs we all have to experience inclusion, safety, and affection, ideally to access opportunities to try to grow into the best version of ourselves.

Although this innate desire for inclusion appears to be a simple, straightforward means of balancing our personal desire to live a life of purpose and meaning with the host of demands others routinely make on us, there's a catch most of us miss. You see, the subtle and seemingly innocent way we become part of the group or stay part of the group is by agreeing to trade some measure of our personal freedom for inclusion into the group. This is why we have such things as vows, oaths, pledges, creeds, and contracts. All of these serve as tangible ways to show we belong to something (such as a club) or someone (such as your spouse), or that we are committed to a particular mission, cause, service, or product (think of your job).

Admittedly, this is not a bad thing—at least not initially. But the real problem arises when the pressures to conform to what others are asking or expecting of us and our own values begin to collide. *This is when we're faced with making a critical choice.* We can either stand fast in our truth, those personal values and fundamental beliefs that represent the basic building blocks of our character, and *risk* no longer feeling accepted or included by others. Or, we can begin giving away even more of our personal power and authority, freely surrendering our truth in order to avoid doing something that could put us in a position to be disinvited to belong because we are deemed to be *different.*

It is at this critical juncture that things can quickly stop being productive and start getting potentially destructive for us. You see, our personal truths represent the ideals and standards we use to direct our behavior. They form the bedrock of the decision-making process we use to make judgments about what we will and will not do when facing an opportunity to act. So when the pressure to conform to what others are expecting or demanding of us begins to supplant our own sense of what's right and wrong, leading us to go against our better judgment or disregard what our values are telling us is the right thing to do in that moment, watch out. We've fallen into the same sad trap as those at Jonestown did—a trap that can quickly set us up to lose everything in life that truly has value.

Loss of Truth

A bedrock principle on which western civilization rests is the primacy of truth. Without a desire for and appreciation of truth, society cannot sustain itself. Take away truth, and one is left without honor, justice, or

NOTE

*Truth is the glue
that holds a sane
and civilized
society together*

decency. Truth is the moral glue that holds a sane and civilized society together.

Remove the former and the latter will crumble.

Exercising the courage to stand your ground when your truth is inconvenient to those around you certainly isn't easy. In fact, over the past thousand years, a whole host of forces around us have sought to influence and shape our personal sense of truth.

From the medieval period through the Renaissance, truth was largely defined by the church. From the Enlightenment to the twentieth century, truth became less connected to faith and more about making sense of our surroundings through reason. In this era, science dethroned theology and today, truth gets largely defined by culture and social context. In other words, it's viewed by many as largely subjective—leaving it up to the individual to create their own version of truth based on the influences they permit into their lives.

Because we live in such a fast-paced society that demands we make a host of choices every day, we understandably can use some help in making sense of all that is happening around us. After all, we want to make choices we believe are good for us, just as we all want to do things that reinforce purpose and meaning in our lives. But here's where things start to unwind if we are not careful.

Given the dynamic nature of the world in which we live, a slew of sources around us—media, religion, politics, and people—are all too happy to help do our thinking for us. Promising the possibility of a happier, thinner, funnier, richer, more powerful, persuasive, or successful you, many employ clever gimmicks, slick slogans, and any other means they can to feed our innate human desire to feel loved, appreciated, or accepted as part of something bigger than ourselves (remember my earlier point about our strong desire to belong to groups). But the more we allow other people's truth to displace our own, the more dangerous things become. And before we know it, our own sense of truth gets watered down or altogether lost, resulting in:

Comfort replacing conviction;
Conformity distorting character; and
Convenience displacing courage.

All of which leave us ill equipped and underprepared to do what we can, when we can, where we can to reject mediocrity and do our part to be a force for good in our part of the world when others need us most.

Haunted by Truth

The absence of truth, represented in those foundational values and beliefs we use to form our attitudes and ultimately shape our actions, has contributed to many of the greatest tragedies in history, the most notorious being the Nazi plan to exterminate the Jewish people in World War II.

As obviously tragic as this dark moment in history was, one question begs to be answered: "How could something like this be allowed to happen?" The answer, unfortunately, is quite simple. Hindsight has shown that the world largely *ignored* what was happening. Be it out of fear, shame, guilt, or a host of other convenient excuses, history confirms the majority of people chose to dismiss the warning signs pointing to the Nazi leadership's evil scheme and simply chose to look the other way. In other words, they knew the truth of what was happening and they opted to ignore it.

At a time when character was needed, both individually and collectively, humanity was largely found wanting.

Author Erwin Lutzer, recounting an eyewitness account of a man who regularly attended a local German church during these troubling times, candidly shares how he and others in his congregation chose to deal with the reality of what they knew was happening around them:

We heard stories of what was happening to the Jews, but we tried to distance ourselves from it, because we felt, what could anyone do to stop it? Each Sunday morning, we would hear the train whistle blowing in the distance, then the wheels coming over the tracks. We became disturbed when we heard cries from the train as it passed by. We realized that it was carrying Jews like cattle in cars!

Week after week the whistle would blow. We dreaded to hear the sounds of those wheels because we knew that we would hear the cries of the Jews enroute to a death camp. Their screams tormented us.

We knew the time the train was coming, and when we heard the whistle blow we began singing hymns. By the time the train came past our church, we were singing at the top of our voices. If we heard the screams, we sang more loudly and soon we heard them no more.

Years have passed and no one talks about it now, but I still hear the train whistle in my sleep.[118]

Of the many things this sad, sobering story can teach us, I find one of the most important is that truth is not something we can hide from. Yes, we can choose to look the other way, convincing ourselves something is not what it really is in that moment or tricking ourselves into *believing* we can somehow justify not standing up and fighting for that which we know in our hearts is worth fighting for. But as this man's candid recounting of his choices confirm, if we fail to exercise the courage to consistently live by our values, our personal sense of truth, then we too will be eventually be subject to the whistle of our own conscience.

There just is no escaping truth.

Cowardly Lion Syndrome

Not long ago our nation witnessed firsthand what happens when we quit fighting for our personal sense of truth. We experienced a phenomenon I've dubbed the *Cowardly Lion Syndrome*.

The situation occurred at a prominent American university. An institution that for generations has been seen as a pillar of integrity and accountability suddenly found itself at the heart of a national controversy that shook it to its foundation.

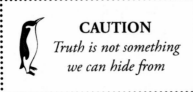

CAUTION
*Truth is not something
we can hide from*

It happened without warning or mercy.

The controversy arose due to allegations that a former school assistant football coach engaged in inappropriate acts with a child on school grounds, and various coaching staff members were aware of it but apparently failed to report the incident to the police. Of course, it's impossible to understand all that really transpired. But one cannot help but wonder what those involved were thinking, and why they didn't do something to curtail what is by any measure, a heinous, criminal act? Perhaps it was fear of damage to the school's reputation if the story went public? Or maybe concern over a lawsuit? Regardless of the logic that contributed to their poor decision, what's clear today is that one or more of the school's leaders failed to exercise the moral courage to act justly in the face of injustice. No one stepped up in defense of a young boy who was effectively defenseless. And although the world may never know the full details of what happened at that venerable institution during that troubling time, we can all learn a valuable lesson from this unfortunate event. Namely that there will certainly be times in life where we will face challenging choices—choices which could lead to our potentially losing something important to us, be it time, position, a relationship, or even prestige. But we must not forget that the true measure of our courage is judged not only by what we do, but equally by what we fail to do when others need our help the most.

Parting Thoughts

On June 12, 1964, Nelson Mandela was sentenced to life in prison in the Republic of South Africa. Refusing to succumb to the falsehood of apartheid, an established social norm that made it acceptable to separate and segregate people based on their race, Mandela went into confinement clinging to the only true hope he had left: *truth*. Twenty-six years later, he emerged from prison, set free by none other than what he valued most in his life: *truth*.

Shortly after his release from prison, South African President F. W. de Klerk and Mandela reached an agreement that would help mend the long-standing rift in their country. And finally, on February 2, 1990, the dark veil of apartheid was lifted from South Africa, forever.

Despite much rejoicing, many questions lingered. Most related to how the deep wounds of so many years of exploitation and hatred could be healed; people questioned how justice could be restored, how reconciliation could be achieved.

To some, only one answer seemed logical. Harkening back to an earlier time in world history where atrocities and heartache met the tribunals of justice in the halls of Nuremberg, Germany, following World War II, the courtroom seemed the most appropriate place to settle the score. But Nelson Mandela, joined by his friend Desmond Tutu, knew they needed to lead their country on a different path. And why not? After all, their entire lives were marked by fighting for truth, sacrificing for truth, and ultimately they were both liberated by truth. In their hearts they knew revenge was not only hollow, but it would do nothing to kick start the process of positive change for the nation and its people.[119]

> **NOTE**
>
> *If we choose inaction when action is clearly warranted, we confirm we don't possess the moral courage to fight for what's right when others need us most*

So, instead of fixating on retaliation, they sought reconciliation. Where retribution would only further divide and move people further apart, they believed restoration would unite and bring people closer together. So, in an incredible act of unwavering commitment to leading the change they wanted to see in their surroundings, these leaders chose to deviate from expectations and create the Truth and Reconciliation Commission. All those who would come forward and confess the truth about their apartheid crimes would be set free. They would be granted instant pardon; amnesty was their gift for the taking.

In the history of modern times, perhaps no act of moral courage stands out so clearly or as profoundly as in this one moment. But it was only made possible because of the conviction of two men of resolute character. Leaders whose commitment to operate in the spirit of the willing burden bearer by making a stand for their deeply held ideals and values ensured truth had her most powerful hour.

And the world has never been the same since.

How might things be different in our society today if more leaders chose to consistently say no to the Cowardly Lion Syndrome and yes to living courageously, regardless of the potential cost to self? How would our own lives change if we became ever more careful not to allow other people's truths to become our own?

Think about it. If you're willing to fight for something—to take a stand, to risk going first, to lead the way in defending what you believe in—then it's fair to say you must value it. And if you value it, then you must be ready to draw your line of personal responsibility around it. Please never forget that the real battle for positive progress is waged with actions. Just like a war of words between nations isn't really a war until soldiers are deployed and placed in harm's way, fighting for what's right in your life really doesn't happen until you start doing something to shape the outcomes you desire.

How does this play out in practical terms? If you want to fight for health, for example, start by exercising or recommitting to your diet. If you want to fight for integrity, then find an opportunity and hold your ground. Speak your mind, live your truth, be your best you—consistently committing to fighting for what's right, be it for yourself or for others, requires conviction; just as accepting responsibility for leading the change you want to see demands courage. Neither happens by chance. Both happen by choice.

And only you can make that choice.

History shows that the only way we can expect to improve things in our surroundings is to risk thinking differently, acting boldly, and dong something to transform our desire to become the best version of ourselves into meaningful action. As the late Dale Carnegie once shared, "Inaction breeds doubt and fear. Action breeds confidence and courage. If you want to conquer fear, do not sit home and think about it. Go out and get busy." Remember, courage is like a muscle. If we push ourselves to exercise it in situations of relatively small consequences, we'll be better equipped when the need to exercise courage in serious situations arise.

So what are we waiting for?

The Fifth Choice

EMBRACE CHANGE...
BE HOPEFUL

Here lies the secret to mastering the psychology of uncertainty:
Never underestimate the power of the human spirit.
—Price Pritchett

Chapter 13

Facing Your Fear of Change

Change before you have to.
—Jack Welch

L ord Horatio Nelson was considered a brave and innovative
leader who was entrusted with the main British battle fleet at
the beginning of the seventeenth century. At a time when a
nation's military might and worldly prestige was largely measured by
the strength of its navy, the widely respected admiral was charged with
finding and destroying Britain's chief rivals, the combined Spanish and
French battle fleets.

This was no small task by any measure, as both nations possessed
impressive capabilities and an equally strong desire to dominate the
seas. Nonetheless, Lord Nelson and his twenty-seven-ship armada set
sail in search of their adversary in the summer of 1805. Departing
English waters in the direction of the West Indies, they located their
enemy several weeks later off the coast of Spain.[120] What was to ensue,
known today as the Battle of Trafalgar, changed the course of naval
history forever.

During this particular time period, traditional naval battles were conducted by engaging ships forming a "line of battle." This tactic prescribed that ships sail parallel to one another, exchanging fire along the way, often at very close range. At times, the vessels engaged in combat would draw so close together that hand-to-hand combat ensued between the crews. This approach to naval warfare was highly predictable and, as a result, very controllable. The comfort of closely following tradition and scripting the conditions of battle provided the captains and their crews with a perceived sense of security.

Familiarity was preferred to adaptability, conformity to ingenuity; mediocrity to imagination.

Lord Nelson, however, was an unconventional leader who understood that blindly following this expected approach left him and his fleet with some very real disadvantages. Most notably, in addition to the Spanish and French possessing numerical superiority (thirty-three vessels to his twenty-seven), their ships were also heavier and carried larger guns than the British vessels. This made it possible for them to deliver more "weight of metal," which was the amount of firepower one ship could bring to bear on another as they sailed alongside their opponent.[121]

Of course, the English ships had unique strengths of their own, which Lord Nelson believed, if properly leveraged, could help him and his crews achieve an unlikely victory. In particular, he recognized that British vessels were not only lighter but were led by more highly skilled sailors than those of their adversary. Additionally, he recognized his men were more disciplined and his gun crews better trained which, when taken together, translated into their being able to fire more rapidly and more accurately than their rivals' ships.[122]

Despite these very real advantages, Lord Nelson recognized the tightly scripted method of warfare would work solidly against them. Thus, to succeed in battle, he and his men would have to change the rules of the game, willfully *deviating* from what was widely accepted in order to try something no one had ever tried before.

And that's exactly what they did.

Charting a Path to Victory

The day before the battle, Lord Nelson convened a meeting with all his ship captains and proposed a bold, creative plan of attack. Instead of attacking in the traditional "line of battle" approach the enemy expected, the British fleet would attempt the unthinkable. They would attack perpendicularly to the enemy's line.

It was a radical idea fraught with both peril and possibilities.

Although this surprising move clearly exposed his vessels to the enemy's superior firepower for a short period of time, it also provided an opportunity to change the rules of engagement in their favor. This allowed them to break down the enemy's planned battle formation into a smaller series of ship-to-ship skirmishes that would leverage the British navy's greatest strengths: superior maneuverability and higher rate of fire.[123]

During the pre-battle meeting aboard the admiral's flagship, HMS *Victory*, Lord Nelson was careful to discuss the plan in detail, soliciting ideas and input from his captains on how to best synchronize the events of the following day. Recognizing that once the battle started there would be little to no chance for communication between the leaders of the various British vessels, the group worked through the counterintuitive tactics and procedures they would employ to pull off this bold action. Every member of Lord Nelson's armada clearly understood that the only way they could achieve such a feat was for every person to set aside the fear of change and give the full measure of their unique strengths to the collective effort at hand.

On the day of the battle, the British plan went off as expected. The French and Spanish ships were so confused by their foe's strange tactics that they did not quite know how to respond. And while most of the English vessels suffered some damage during the battle and Lord Nelson himself was killed, not a single British ship was lost. Conversely, the combined French and Spanish fleet lost some twenty vessels to capture, explosion, fire, or scuttling.

The result of the now famous Battle of Trafalgar proved a major victory for the British forces that forever changed the way future naval engagements would be fought. And it was all made possible because of a leader who was willing to create the conditions for others to flourish and thrive. A leader whose selfless actions two-hundred years ago teaches us even today that we are at our best when we choose to see change as an opportunity, not as an obstacle; to recognize it as a potential friend rather than an almost certain foe.

Change Is Here to Stay

Ask anyone in business, or the military, or education, or any field, for that matter, and one thing you will invariably hear is that effectively dealing with change is one of, if not the, single biggest challenge facing all of us today. This, of course, is not a revelation. In fact, volumes have been written about the need for change. But for all the times we hear these words, few of us recognize we are only hearing half the story. You see, speaking about the need for change infers change is a one-time event being driven by a certain shift in circumstances or posed by a particular problem. The reality, however, is that change is a natural byproduct of life on earth. It's an ever-present requirement if we are intent to become the best version of ourselves possible.

> **WARNING**
> *Cognitive scientists have found that when it comes to our initial reaction toward change, our brains are actually wired to work against us*

Think about this truth in relation to the example of Lord Nelson. How might things have been different if he chose to continue to use the same old strategy to engage a numerically superior adversary? Well, I'm no navy genius, but I can do simple math. If you are outgunned and outmanned, you know the way things have always been done will very likely not net the result you desire. Essentially this leaves only two possible choices: either roll the dice and hope things work out okay, or accept responsibility for challenging established convention and commit to *doing something different* in order to try to proactively influence outcomes in your surroundings. The choice is yours and yours alone.

Or is it?

As it turns out, cognitive scientists have found that when it comes to our initial reaction toward change, *our brains are actually wired to work against us.* So much so, in fact, that these same scientists have determined our initial resistance to change is actually *a primal instinct.* A natural by-product of how we are *neurologically* wired as human beings. And though scores of books have been written listing the reasons why we avoid change, too few highlight that the real culprit is *our own thinking.*[124]

So let's set out to change that, beginning now.

The Status Quo Bias

Several years ago, the German government undertook a strip-mining project that required (by law) that a small town be relocated. At its own expense, the government offered to rebuild the town in a different location and compensate the citizens for their trouble. Urban planning specialists offered innovative ideas to the local population about how their new surroundings could be designed and configured to make it more modern, state of the art, and convenient for the townspeople than their current arrangement. But ultimately, the citizens refused the scores of creative options and progressive advice of the engineers and experts, choosing instead a plan extraordinarily similar to the highly inefficient, serpentine design of their existing city. In the end, despite facing an unprecedented opportunity to dramatically improve their current state of affairs, the town population's discomfort with change ensured the status quo prevailed.[125]

The willingness to change remains one of humanity's oldest dilemmas and, as such, has given birth to the major sciences whose texts now fill the world's libraries. Business managers seek to harness the power of change to maximize value for their shareholders. Marketers seek to understand what prompts one to change from Coke to Pepsi, Nike to Reebok. Psychiatrists and psychologists have developed thousands upon thousands of theories on what practices, therapies, and remedies can best help people navigate change and achieve new levels of wholeness and happiness in the process.[126] Yet, any way you look at it, change, and the uncertainty that accompanies change, is unpleasant and often downright unwelcome for one primary reason: it invokes fear in us. And when our hearts and minds are full of fear, science confirms that our natural human response is to do everything we can to reduce, if not outright eliminate, the source of discomfort we're experiencing in our current circumstances.

One of the primary ways our body tries to keep us safe in those fearful situations is to trigger a little-known *psychological* self-preservation mechanism scientist and psychologists term *the status-quo bias.*

Researchers confirm that "the source of the status quo bias lies deep within our psyches, in our desire to protect our egos from damage. Breaking from the status quo means taking action, and when we take action, we take responsibility, thus opening ourselves to criticism and to regret."[127] Given we as humans don't like experiencing loss or regret or anything that will significantly upset our present realities, the status-quo bias kicks in to automate decision making at every opportunity—taking things we learn and making them second nature.[128]

Now this makes sense at one level. After all, why should we have to keep learning the same things over and over again if we can learn it once or twice and then develop a simple default option that makes future choices simple, automatic, and ultimately more efficient? But here's the problem. When we are confronted with something that doesn't fit neatly into what we've come to expect, this well-intentioned process starts working against us. Now, instead of warnings spurring us to action, the status-quo bias *directs us to keep doing things the same old way.* Unconsciously convincing us it's better to cling to our familiar routines than venture forward into the unknown.[129]

WARNING
Despite being a biological mechanism to help make life easier for us, the status-quo bias actually trips us up

In practical terms, this ever-present bias toward preserving the existing state of affairs helps explain why we routinely do such things as eat the same foods, visit the same stores, talk to the same people, buy the same products, obsess over the same thoughts, and return to the same vacation spots. It also helps us understand why so many people prefer to stay with an investment strategy or maintain a particular financial portfolio, even when they are losing money.

Despite being a biological mechanism to help make life easier for us, the status-quo bias routinely trips us up. It convinces us we are better off to be like the West German villagers and stick with the familiarity of "the way we've always done it around here." So what can we do to short circuit this invisible tendency to accept mediocrity as the norm? Quite simply, change our focus. Instead of fixating on what might go wrong by stepping outside our comfort zone, we should focus on what may go right if we use our unique strengths to risk moving out in a new direction.

Share Our Strength

On a hot and hazy morning in August 1984, Bill Shore, a senior political advisor to Senator Gary Hart, had no idea that life as he knew it was about to significantly change. Coming off the sudden, unexpected collapse of Hart's presidential campaign, Shore sat quietly reading the *Washington Post* when he came across a brief article about impending famine in Africa: "200,000 to Die This Summer in Ethiopia," the headline read. However, what really got Shore's attention was that although the calamity had not yet struck and the experts could see it coming, they confessed they knew nothing would be done to stop it. Much like suddenly turning on a light switch in a darkened room, Shore's mind instantly flooded with images of what he believed could be done to positively influence the situation. "The newspaper story read like an invitation to act," Shore clearly recalls. [130]

And act he did.

Before this moment, "action" would likely have meant recommending some politically beneficial policy or program to the powerful politicians he had worked with for many years. But now, it meant following the impulse to use his talent, imagination, and connections to pull together a network of seemingly disparate causes and purposes, enterprises and individuals, to help lead the change he wanted to see. Several weeks later, Share Our Strength (SOS) was founded.

Taking out a $2,000 cash advance on a credit card, Shore and his sister Debbie rented a row house in Washington D.C. and got to work. They started by developing a simple, straightforward philosophy to guide their efforts: *It takes more than food to fight hunger.* And they've never looked back since.

Today, almost three decades later, they are still going strong. Having raised more than $315 million dollars to help reach their goal of eliminating hunger and its primary accomplice, poverty, they've positively influenced millions of people across the globe—their success in making such a meaningful difference in society a by-product of their willingness to pursue an unconventional approach to serving some of the most vulnerable citizens on our planet.[131]

You see, unlike other not-for-profit organizations working to serve humanity who rely largely on donations or government grants to accomplish their mission, Share Our Strength doesn't ask others to give money. Instead they focus on creating innovative opportunities for people to share the best of *themselves.* They engage common leaders such as chefs, writers, musicians, lawyers, bankers, scientists, artists— many previously uninvolved and uncommitted—and ask them to share their energy, talents, and deepest passion to help support a cause worth fighting for.[132]

For instance, writers are encouraged to contribute their writing; chefs to donate food, specialty dishes, and cooking skills; and business executives are asked to share their expertise in strategic planning, marketing, and communication. In Shore's own words, "Ours is an organization of ordinary people putting food in front of others who have no food—people leaving their homes or offices to teach, train, and befriend others in neighborhoods where there are no such homes or offices; people using their restaurants, hotels, public relations firms, printing companies, photography darkrooms, or breweries to produce the dollars needed to staff kitchens, shelters, and health clinics."[133] Their success proving firsthand how the solutions to our society's most pressing problems already exists, invisible in plain sight, in the example of everyday leaders willing to say no to the status quo and yes to promoting positive progress—one opportunity at a time.[134]

Balanced Strengths

As the wide-felt impact of Share Our Strength confirms, people and organizations thrive when they are free to choose the nature and extent of their contribution. This suggests that treating people like *volunteers* in the process of positive change—with freedom to choose to contribute as they most desire—helps to bypass our natural fear of change by unleashing both our personal and collective strength.

Admittedly, the concept of focusing on our strengths as a means of bringing out the best of ourselves and those around us is not an uncommon concept. Nor should it be as promoting positive qualities is such an appealing notion. After all, who wants to hear about shortcomings or much less spend energy trying to fix them when change is already so difficult? Why not just focus on what works well and stay away from what doesn't feel natural or makes us feel uncomfortable?

Here's the challenge with this notion. Although building on strength is preferred, ignoring those things in our lives that are not working as they should will not make them go away. Nor will it negate the toll it will take on our effectiveness. As Tony Schwartz points out in a recent Harvard Business Review blog post, "...narrowing attention to the preferred aspects of ourselves vastly oversimplifies who we are, what stands in our way, and what it takes to operate at our best."[135]

What Schwartz is pointing out is the fact that an overused strength eventually turns into a liability. He adds, "The missteps we make and the damage we inflict on others is less the result of failing to fully utilize our strengths and more the consequence of overvaluing and over-relying on them—precisely because they come more easily to us."[136]

I know this all too well myself. One of my strengths is passion for what I'm doing. Give me a project and I will dive into it tenaciously and enthusiastically. And although it's certainly important to believe in what you're doing, I've learned over the years that untempered

CAUTION
Although building on strength is preferred, ignoring those things in our lives that are not working as they should will not make them go away

enthusiasm can quickly become overbearing. It also can wear people down physically and emotionally as not everyone shares the same level of excitement for a particular cause, campaign, or endeavor.

The remedy, you ask? In my case it's not necessarily reducing my passion for what I'm doing, it's appropriately focusing it. Too much sober moderation, after all, leads to boring blandness. What I've needed to learn—and continue to learn—is how infusing my energy when and where it's needed most to keep the effort moving forward, especially when progress gets bogged down or when we experience an unexpected setback, is what adds the greatest value to my surroundings in that moment.

Don't forget, our nation doesn't need leaders who think they have all the answers. Rather, we need leaders who are aware of their strengths and courageous enough to acknowledge their shortcomings. It's a paradoxical challenge we all face: to hold ourselves accountable for doing what we can to grow into the best version of ourselves while accepting ourselves exactly as we are along the way.

Parting Thoughts

One of the real tragedies with allowing our fear of change to hold us back from stretching our abilities and exploring the extent of our capabilities is that we may never come to realize just how powerful we really are. Much like an elephant that, little by little, is slowly lulled into surrendering their strength without ever putting up a fight, we too often fail to realize all we are capable of doing or achieving

Think about the truth of this metaphor in your own life.

An elephant trainer does not subdue an elephant all at once. He can't. The elephant is too big, too strong, and maybe even (at first) too stubborn. But the trainer, wise in his ways, first secures the young elephant with a mighty chain, hitched to a sturdy, formidable post. As the elephant grows larger, the trainer replaces the chain with a weaker tether, such as a rope, secured this time to a stake. When the elephant is mature, the rope is eventually replaced with string, secured to something as flimsy as a blade of grass. Although the full-grown elephant certainly possesses the power to escape, he long ago quit resisting. He's now trapped by an imaginary chain, wrought from his limited thinking and old ways of being that hold him back from experiencing the life he desires and deserves.[137]

The status-quo bias serves as the proverbial string in our own lives that keeps us from thinking and acting for ourselves. Robbing our freedom of movement only because we allow it to, the string keeps us anchored firmly in the present. And when our present circumstances are all we care to see; our fear of the future and fascination with familiarity lead us to freely surrender our unique strength without even thinking twice.

When this becomes routine, then ordinary becomes acceptable.

Complacency becomes comfortable.

And stretching toward our potential is altogether avoided.

Making it easy for a mediocre me mindset to convince us to lead a life far smaller, shallower, and narrower than we are each capable of living.

Chapter 14

Make Hope a Habit

Optimism is the faith that leads to achievement.
Nothing can be done without hope and confidence.
—Helen Keller

Deep in the jungle, on the banks of the slow-moving Kwai Noi River, simple bronze headstones solemnly mark the graves of 1,740 heroes. The great men memorialized in this remote stretch of jungle were members of several allied nations' armed services who perished as prisoners of war in Japanese labor camps during World War II. These brave soldiers, sailors, airmen, and marines died building and maintaining the infamous Thailand-Burma railway.[138]

Sadly, more than half of the two hundred thirty thousand POWs who built the "Death Railway," as it became known, gave their lives in the process—a POW lost for every railroad tie laid. By night these men struggled to survive the squalor of labor camps, while by day they were marched out to suffer in the jungle's intense heat and humidity. Some died as they worked and were buried in the riverbanks of the jungle where they fell, their graves marked solely by bottles holding their nametags.

Most, however, died in the shabby prison camps themselves. Exhausted from work and overcome by starvation, they became, in their own words, "living skeletons."[139]

The prisoners of one such camp, known simply as Camp Number Two in Chungkai, Thailand, lived lives of especially unimaginable horror. Positioned deep within the jungle, the harshness of the environment was overshadowed only by the heartlessness of their enemy. An enemy equally bent on breaking the soldiers' spirits as they were destroying their bodies.

Yet, despite their difficult and discouraging conditions, the prisoners actively sought opportunities to build value into one another's lives. Be it sharing an encouraging word, helping another person complete their assigned task, or simply providing a reassuring glance when someone was struggling, they did what they could, when they could, where they could to communicate their support to one another.

After many months of psychological and physical abuse, however, the will of the prisoners began to break down. Now routinely fighting for food and stealing from friends, the law of the jungle became the norm in the camp. Dignity began to be displaced by despair, and the original commitment to "What can I do for another?" degenerated into a growing sense of "How can I save myself?"

The guards sensed that they were succeeding in breaking the will of the prisoners and were all too pleased to help each man descend deeper into their own hopeless, lonely place. In time, they even found they no longer needed the three-by-three-foot crates for solitary confinement; one by one, each person succeeded in isolating themselves in their own misery. Though more than ten thousand men were crowded together in a very small space, each felt increasingly alone as their sense of hope steadily slipped away.

And then, almost instantly, everything changed.

Sparks of Hope

Two new prisoners to the camp, Colonel Edward "Weary" Dunlop and Captain Ernest Gordon, arrived. They brought with them a *hope-full* focus and contagious commitment to being a force for good in their part of the world. They started small at first, sharing meals or offering a compassionate ear. When men struggled to complete their assigned duties, they offered to finish the job. Bandaging bruises, washing wounds, or scraping sores, these men actively accepted responsibility for making a positive difference in their surroundings.

Colonel Dunlop quickly set out to transform the bamboo hut that once served as the camp's "death ward" into a hospital, enlisting medical assistants to join him in providing a much-needed prescription of hope to even the most broken of prisoners. Meanwhile, Captain Gordon sought new ways to reach out to others, becoming the camp's unofficial chaplain. Repeatedly defying stern warning from the guards, he even opened a makeshift open-air church, organized an education system, and formed an orchestra and a theater.[140]

Slowly and insidiously, the positive example of the newcomers began to change those around them. And for the first time in a long while, prisoners began to once again act like comrades. Their selfishness transformed by selflessness, the men found new eyes through which to see their situation in a different light. And although their physical conditions had not been altered, something within them did.

They had rediscovered hope in one another.[141]

What Is Hope?

It's been said that hope is the first of our "emergency" virtues. Specifically, hope is a virtue that keeps us going through difficulties. It is a life raft we cling to when all seems lost.

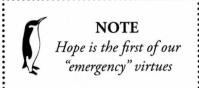

NOTE
Hope is the first of our "emergency" virtues

History repeatedly reminds us that a leader's ability to generate hope is one of the greatest force multipliers known to mankind. Be it on battlefields or in boardrooms, classrooms or emergency rooms, it is hope that often spells the difference between success and failure, between achieving an acceptable outcome and an exceptional performance, and sometimes, as we see in the example of the prisoners of Camp Number Two, hope may even prove to be the difference between life and death.

The dictionary tells us hope means "to look forward to with confidence or expectation."[142] From such a view, hope encourages us to adopt an *optimistic* vision of the future that is much better than the status quo. It enables us to claim our power when we feel powerless, just as it empowers us to transcend our limitations when we feel we don't have what it takes to grow into our fullest potential. Thus, in simplest terms, *hope helps us defeat mediocrity by pointing our imagination in a positive direction.*

Of course, this does not imply hope is a denial of reality. Nor is it an elixir to cure all of our ills. We can, after all, hope for a job, for success for our family, for recovery from illness, for a better, safer world. But hope certainly comes with no guarantees. Rather, it is, in the words of Joan Chittister, "…a series of small actions that transforms darkness into light. It is putting one foot in front of the other when we can find no reason to do so at all."[143] Hope then is where we turn when we have no sure answers but still yearn for a better end. It is hope, as the *Stockdale Paradox* we'll soon explore confirms, which allows us to overcome hurdles we could not otherwise endure and, in doing so, moves us into a space where healing and growth can begin to occur.

The Stockdale Paradox

Admiral James Stockdale, a decorated war hero and former vice presidential candidate, was shot down in Vietnam and imprisoned in the "Hanoi Hilton" for almost eight years. As the senior ranking officer, he was tortured more than twenty times by his captors, and never had much reason to believe he would survive the prison camp and someday get to see his wife and family again. And yet, Stockdale recalls he never lost *hope* during his ordeal: "I never doubted not only that I would get out, but also that I would prevail in the end and turn the experience into the defining event of my life, which, in retrospect, I would not trade."[144]

As he relays in his book, *In Love and War*, Stockdale's ability to endure the difficult, daunting, and often discouraging circumstances around him stemmed from his deeply held belief that "you must maintain absolute faith that you will prevail while recognizing the brutal reality of your current situation." In other words, the Stockdale Paradox reminds us we must retain a *hopeful* outlook but protect ourselves from adopting unrealistic expectations.

WARNING
The tendency to be more optimistic than realistic is a common trap people tend to fall into

Stockdale shares how it was always the most overly optimistic of his prison mates who failed to make it out of the Vietnamese POW camp alive: "They were the ones who said, 'We're going to be out by Christmas.' And Christmas would come, and Christmas would go. Then they'd say, 'We're going to be out by Easter.' And Easter would come, and Easter would go. And then Thanksgiving, and then it would be Christmas again. And they died of a broken heart."[145]

Emerging research in the fields of neuroscience and social science suggests that the tendency to be more optimistic than realistic is a common trap people tend to fall into. This belief that the future will be much better than the past is known as the *optimism bias* and exists in every race, region and socioeconomic bracket. And although possessing a positive perspective can certainly help us continue to press forward when a situation gets tough, where this thought process gets us into particular trouble is when our overly positive assumptions lead to disastrous miscalculations—convincing us to hinge our future hopes on a fantasy far removed from anything we can expect to reasonably occur.[146]

Thus, the Stockdale Paradox reminds us that to be effective as leaders, our hopeful outlooks must both be tempered by a tenacious realism and activated by a dose of *defensive pessimism*—a way of looking at the world that equips us to balance our optimistic desires for the future with a healthy dose of eyes-wide-open pessimism in the present.[147]

Shoes or No Shoes?

"Have you heard the story of the two shoe salesmen? Two guys from two different companies fly into a remote part of Africa where they encounter a tribe that has never seen shoes, let alone worn them. One salesman immediately calls his headquarters and says, "Stop the order. Nobody here wears shoes. We can't sell anything!" The other salesman calls his boss and says, "Triple the order. Nobody here wears shoes. We can sell a pair to everyone!"[148]

Chet McDoniel loves telling this story as a way to prompt people to consider how often they've chosen to see a situation only from a negative perspective. His words serving as a reminder how every circumstance, no matter how fraught with adversity, also offers an opportunity for us to stretch and grow closer to becoming the best version of ourselves possible.

Admittedly, at first brush this may sound like common advice. Easy to say, but challenging to do. But have I mentioned that Chet was born without arms and with shortened legs? Enough adversity to frustrate anyone—anyone but Chet, it seems.

In his book *I'm Not Broken*, he relays the story of how his parents initially saw nothing but heartbreak and devastation when Chet was born. They loved him as any parent loves a child, but an overwhelming sense of hopelessness initially engulfed them, as it likely would any parent facing such a significant challenge.

Many nights passed with Chet's mother and father positioned over their son's crib, eyes filled with tears and hearts filled with hurt as they envisioned what the future would likely hold for a child with no arms and only partial legs. But this attitude did not last long. One day, while Chet was still a baby, his parents decided it was time for a change, so they committed to raising their son as they would any other child.

From that day forward they choose to willfully instill in him a sense of hopeful optimism tempered with an eyes-wide-open dose of defensive pessimism. As he grew from a teen into a young man, they continued to encourage Chet to continue pursue his dream of becoming a worship leader. All the while reminding him how success could prove an elusive experience.

Chet shares, "When I decided to become a worship minister, I was full of ambition and motivation. I sent my résumé to every church where I thought my style would fit. I was interviewed by many, but once I mentioned my handicap, the tone of the interview changed. I usually didn't hear back from them." Although these repeated rejections were certainly discouraging, he adds how he did not allow these short-term disappointments to sap his strength or steal his hope. Making it a point to "walk a mile" in the shoes of the interviewers, he recognized his physical limitations were an obstacle many people just couldn't bring themselves to look past. Nonetheless, he adds "I made a conscious decision to keep pressing on. I sent out more résumés and finally a small church in Irving, Texas, brought me in for an interview. I auditioned the following Sunday by leading worship in the morning service and was hired that day."

Despite facing what many would consider almost insurmountable odds, Chet finally attained his dream. His tenacity undoubtedly aided by the fact that he chose to temper his series of disappointments with an indomitable belief that this latest setback was only temporary—just another way to demonstrate his commitment to leading his life in a more excellent way—one opportunity a time.

Today, Chet is married and has a daughter of his own. In addition to leading worship, motivational speaking, and owning his own travel agency, he also graduated magna cum laude from the University of North Texas and continues to deliver his message of hope and happiness to thousands of people every year—ever thankful he never allowed mediocrity to become an acceptable response, no matter how challenging things around him became.[149]

Practicing Defensive Pessimism

As the amazing story of Chet McDoniel illustrates, hope is an emotional force for good that points our imagination towards positive things. In the words of Price Pritchett, hope "energizes and mobilizes us, serving as a catalyst for action. Because hope links directly to our confidence levels, it inspires us to aim higher, put forth more effort, and have more staying power."[150] As this description aptly portrays, hope certainly packs a powerful positive punch.

> **WARNING**
> *Hopelessness clouds the way we look at things, making us suspicious of the future and negative about the present*

But for all the attention placed on the value of practicing unrestrained optimism, a more nuanced view is emerging from the laboratory. One which now shows, as Annie Paul writes in a recent edition of *Psychology Today*, how balancing our optimism with a healthy dose of defensive pessimism can insulate us from experiencing crushing disappointment when things don't go our way.[151] This speaks to what Admiral Stockdale was describing in the case of the heartbroken prisoners whose excessive hopefulness led them to die in captivity, often of shattered spirits.[152] Conversely, Stockdale and the others who survived understood that adopting a more balanced outlook actually helps protect us from experiencing undue emotional hardship or excessive heartache should things not unfold as we have dreamed, planned, or imagined they would.

The key, of course, to making this approach work for us is to learn to match the mindset to the situation. For example, in times of great uncertainty or significant change that demands we take some form of risk, such as starting our own business, optimism is the ticket. After all, optimism motivates people to work as hard as they possibly can on their long-shot ventures, effectively buffering them from the ever-present risk of failure. But when our fears are more concrete and immediate—such as when we think we may receive bad news related to our health, our work, or our relationships, we are wise to temper our optimism.

Kate Sweeny, an assistant professor of psychology at the University of California, Riverside, has found that intentionally bracing ourselves for a negative outcome actually has a *positive* psychological effect. "When you finally get the bad news, you still feel bad, but not as bad as if you never saw it coming," says Sweeny. "You've had a chance to work through the emotional implications of this negative event in advance. You may even have put some supports in place—bringing a friend along to a doctor's appointment, perhaps, to help you cope with a worrisome diagnosis, or lining up a tutor if you know you've failed an important exam."[153]

Optimism and pessimism, it turns out, can be unexpected allies as they give us the courage to stretch outside our comfort zones and try new things. No matter how daunting our circumstances may seem in the moment, when we consciously pause to think through both aspects, the potential good as well as the potential bad that may result from taking a particular action, we strike a powerful balance that gives us an enhanced perspective and renewed confidence to abandon the safety of our familiar routines and head in bold new directions.

Parting Thoughts

"Hope envisages its future and then acts as if that future is now irresistible, thus helping to create the reality for which it longs," says theologian Walter Wink.[154] He adds, "Even a small number of people fully committed to the new inevitability on which they have fixed their imaginations can decisively affect the shape the future takes."[155] In other words, Wink is reminding all of us that we already possess everything we need to reject a mediocre me mindset and get busy positively influencing outcomes in our surroundings.

All we have to do is choose to get off the sideline and into the game.

James McGregor Burns shares in his book, *Transforming Leadership,* how in every arena of life it is natural for human beings to strive to fulfill their personal needs and desires, however

> **NOTE**
>
> *Balancing our optimism with a healthy dose of defensive pessimism… can actually insulate us from experiencing crushing disappointment*

meager or simple they might be. Burns adds that it is a leader who is often best positioned to liberate people to grow into the very best version of themselves by investing in others a sense of possibility, "…a belief that changes can be made and that they can make them." And when this occurs, suddenly, "opportunity beckons where none had appeared before, and once seized upon opens another opportunity and another."[156] From such a perspective then, we are reminded how hope makes our hearts sing and forms the foundation for many a wonderful thing. Hope, however, is not merely an emotion, something we either do or do not possess. Rather, *hope, much like leadership, is first and foremost a choice.* A choice to employ an optimistic outlook while protecting ourselves from developing unrealistic expectations that could ultimately set us up for a disappointing fall.

In September 1945, after the atomic bombs fell on Hiroshima and Nagasaki, World War II came to a close. There were no friendly troops to open the gates for the survivors of Camp Number Two. The guards had silently left, defeated, in the middle of the night. The inmates emerged together to the freedom of a new day. After the war, each man who walked through those prison gates spent the rest of his life knowing his survival was not an individual accomplishment, but a testimony to the power of hope to transform the darkest of circumstances into the most powerful of possibilities.

Hope delivered by a pair of leaders whose example teaches us that although we may at times be afflicted in every way, we need not be crushed; though perplexed, we need not despair. For in choosing to point our imagination toward positive things, we affirm our belief in the age-old Arab proverb that "he who has hope has everything." Everything, that is, needed to see change as an opportunity to defeat mediocrity by pointing our imaginations in a more positive direction.

The Sixth Choice

CHECK YOUR EGO...
BE GRATEFUL

Most powerful is he who has himself in his own power.
—Seneca, Roman Philosopher

Chapter 15

Beware the Ego Trap

I am, indeed, a king, because I know how to rule myself.
—Pietro Aretino

Long ago there lived an island king who one sleepless night, got it into his head that he would like to touch the moon.

"Why not?" he asked himself, "After all, I am the King. What I want, I get. And I want to touch the moon."

The next morning the king called his chief carpenter into the royal court.

"I want you to build me a tower," he commanded. "One tall enough to reach the moon."

The carpenter's stomach jumped and his eyes bulged.

"The moon, sire? Did you say the moon?"

"You heard me. I want to touch the moon. Now go do it!"

The carpenter left the royal court and called a meeting with all the other carpenters. They talked, scratched their heads, and decided his majesty must have been joking. So they built nothing at all.

A few days passed by and the king summoned the chief carpenter back to the royal court.

"I don't see my tower," he barked. "What's taking so long?"

"But your majesty, the carpenter cried, "you can't be serious. A tower to the moon? It's too hard. We don't know how."

"I don't care how you do it, but I want it done and done quickly" the king demanded. "You have three days. If by that time I have not touched the moon, you cannot begin to imagine all the horrible things I'll do to you."

The shaken carpenter ran out of the royal court and again, convened a meeting with his carpenter friends. The assembled carpenters scratched their heads, drew some lines on paper, and racked their brains for an answer. Finally, they came up with a plan.

The chief carpenter quickly went back to the king.

"We have an idea that just might work," he said. "But we'll need every box in the kingdom."

"Excellent!" cried the king. "Let it be done!"

The king sent out a royal decree that every box in the kingdom be carried to the palace. The people brought them in every shape and size— crates and chests and cases and cartons, shoe boxes, hat boxes, flower boxes, even bread boxes.

Then the carpenter ordered that all the boxes be piled one on top of the other, until there wasn't a single box left. But the tower was still not high enough to reach the moon.

"We'll have to make more," he told the king.

So another royal decree was issued. His majesty ordered that every tree on the island be chopped down and the timber brought to the palace. The carpenters made more boxes, adding them to the ever-growing tower.

"I think its high enough," the king announced.

The carpenters looked up nervously.

"Perhaps I should go first...," the chief carpenter suggested. "...Just to be on the safe side."

"Don't be silly!" the king barked. "This was my idea. I will be the first one to touch the moon. The honor belongs to me."

He started to climb. Higher and higher he mounted. He left the birds far below, and broke through the clouds. When he got to the top, he stretched out his arms—but he was just barely short! A few more inches and he would be able to bask in the glory of being the first to touch the moon! Or at least that's the way it looked to him.

"One more box!" he yelled down. "I need just one more box!"

The carpenters just shook their heads. They had already gathered every box and used every piece of wood in the Kingdom.

"We don't have anymore!" they yelled at the top of their lungs. "No more boxes! You'll have to come down now sire."

The king stamped his foot and jumped up and down. The whole tower trembled.

"I won't come down! I won't!" he yelled. "I want to be the first to touch the moon and no one is going to stop me."

Then his majesty, confident he knew more than anyone else about building towers to the moon, had his brilliant idea.

"Listen here," he called. "I know what to do. Take the first box from the bottom and bring it to the top."

The carpenters stared at each other in disbelief.

"You fools!" the king yelled. "You're wasting my time! Take the first box and bring it up now!"

The carpenters shrugged.

"This is a very stubborn and prideful king," the chief carpenter said, "I suppose we must obey his command."

So they pulled out the bottom box.

You don't need to be told the rest of the story.[157]

An Unforgettable Flight

Who reading this has not been exposed to a leader who, much like the self-oriented, box-stacking king, possesses an inaccurate or incomplete view of themselves that primes them for a fall? I know I certainly have.

Many years ago as a young Captain serving as an instructor pilot in a flying organization supporting senior military and civilian leaders, I was told I would be flying with a very high ranking military official. Admittedly, I was slightly intimidated. If not because of his rank and position then surely because he had been flying airplanes longer than I had been alive. And, to add to the mounting anxiety, it surely didn't help that he had previously served as a member of *The Thunderbirds*, the Air Force's elite jet demonstration team.

To make matters more interesting, he also had a reputation for being egotistical and particularly pride-*full*. Nonetheless, I very much looked forward to the opportunity to fly and perhaps briefly visit, with someone who has served our nation for almost four decades.

As expected, it proved to be a memorable flight.

The day arrived and I flew the jet to Andrews AFB in Maryland and awaited the senior leader's arrival. He showed up on time and immediately climbed into the cockpit. No time for pleasantries—no "Hello!" or "How are you?" This man was all business. I thought little of it. After all, he was busy and undoubtedly had a great deal on his mind.

As he pushed the throttles up to begin the short taxi to the runway, I began to brief him on the required takeoff data; weather, winds, and standard takeoff procedures. He nodded his head, grunted something indiscernible and kept taxing…fast. I respectfully asked he slow just a bit to ensure we kept within established guidelines.

Not a good plan.

He turned, glared at me, and then I think he actually sped up!

Fortunately, we were cleared for an immediate takeoff, which at our current taxi speed, wouldn't take us long to achieve. As we rolled down the runway, he noticed an amber light on the enunciator panel in front of him and asked why it was on. I responded it was the nose wheel engaged indicator—a standard reminder to the pilot flying to release the steering switch once they begin their takeoff role.

Now visibly upset that my comment insinuated he had somehow performed below perfection, he released the button and we continued the takeoff uneventfully. Needless to say, it was the quietest and perhaps, most uncomfortable hour long flight of my life. One that left a lasting impression upon me of just how easy it is for our uncontrolled egos to set us up to build our own proverbial towers to the moon.

Eliminating Favorable Bias toward Self

The fact you are reading a book on leadership likely means you, too, possess a decent-sized ego. And that's perfectly okay. After all, a healthy, vibrant, and balanced sense of self-confidence is essential to being an effective leader. .

The problem arises, however, when our ego gets the better of us and begins to distort our perspective of who we are, what we are capable of, and the role others play in both our success and failure. When this occurs, our inflated view of self begins to subtly position us to fall prey to one of the single greatest hindrances to leading our lives in a more excellent way—*pride.*

Pride has perplexed philosophers and theologians for centuries, and is an especially paradoxical emotion in American culture. On the one hand, we applaud rugged individualism, self-reliance and personal excellence. On the other, we understand that too much pride can easily tip the balance toward vanity, selfishness and ultimately, self-destruction.

Pride, however, does not simply hurt us personally. If left unchecked, it corrodes human community and erodes our sense of dependence on one another.[158] In effect, it lulls us into believing we are more talented, capable or successful than we really are.

In a series of fascinating experiments at the University of Florida designed to examine the effects of pride in our lives, Professor Barry Schlenker randomly assigned people to work together as a group on a particular task. Upon completion of the task, he falsely informed each person that his or her group had performed well or poorly. In every one of these studies the members of the successful groups claimed *greater responsibility* for their group's performance than did the member of groups that supposedly failed at the task. Additionally, in the successful groups, almost all of the members claimed personally contributing more to the tasks than their group mates; very few said they contributed less.[159] What this experiment confirmed is how predisposed people are to what Schlenker terms, *"favorable bias toward self,"* which is akin to the phrase often used in Greek drama, *hubris.*

Hubris is a negative term implying arrogant, excessive self-pride or self-confidence that, if not kept in check, leads to someone developing a tragic flaw in their character. Much like the box-stacking king in our earlier story and the unnamed previous military senior leader, hubris blinds us to our own biases—setting us up to take a potentially disastrous fall.

The question then, is how do we guard ourselves from falling into the self-imposed traps our ego's subtly set for us? I have two words for you: *self control.*

Self-Control: The Key to Effectively Managing Self

Admittedly, self-control, otherwise known as temperance, is not popular in today's culture.[160] In fact, it's counter-cultural as much of our society loves to make self-gratification a priority worth pursuing; often at any cost. However, exercising self-control, defined as *the ability to look outside oneself in a way that balances a healthy self-denial with a deep seated commitment to live up to a particular standard,* is what guards us from making irrational or impulsive choices that contribute to our unwittingly falling prey to adopting a favorable bias toward self.[161]

> **NOTE**
> *Self*-control *is the ability to look outside oneself in a way that balances a healthy self-denial with a deep seated commitment to live up to a particular standard*

Be it as simple as staying true to our diet, refusing to succumb to peer pressure or refraining from lashing out at someone who has hurt us deeply, self-control prevents us from caving in to the pressure we all at times face to override rationality or good judgment. This is an important point to consider. After all, as leaders in our homes, workplaces, worship spaces, and communities, we want to make our mark. We want our leadership to be felt. And that's okay. However, the challenge arises when the pressure to perform leads us to make decisions that are more about ourselves than in the best interest of our organizations; our families; our customers; or our constituents. As such, it's quite easy for us to blur the line between pushing forward to grow into the best version of ourselves by pursuing our goals, dreams and aspirations and regulating our ego's appetite for applause, acclaim, and adulation. Let me provide you with one more quick illustration to help further explain this important distinction.[162]

Not long ago I had the privilege of taking part in a conversation with legendary founder and former CEO of Southwest Airlines, Herb Kelleher. The topic of discussion related to why Southwest Airlines, the only airline to remain profitable every year it's been in business, has been so successful while it's one time peer-competitor People Express fizzled out and disappeared after only six years in service. It was a simple enough question that was ultimately met with an even simpler, straightforward answer. Nevertheless, let me give you a little background before I share with you Herb Kelleher's succinct, one-word response as to the source of their one-time competitor's demise.

Originally launched as a low-cost, no-frills airline in 1981, People Express expanded very quickly. In addition to acquiring a number of regional air carriers, including Denver-based Frontier Airlines, they also chose to venture into international air travel.[163] In just four years, People Express went from its founding to being the fifth-largest airline in the nation. It was a meteoric rise and, as history reveals, an equally rapid fall.[164]

Just one year after completing its host of acquisitions, People Express filed for bankruptcy protection. Shortly thereafter, they ceased to exist as an independent carrier.

So what happened?

In simplest terms, the company's CEO became fixated on expanding more and more for fear of being left behind by other major airlines. This led him and his team to acquire a number of competitor airlines simply for the sake of growth, which ultimately led to their amassing a debt load they simply could no longer service. This mountain of unpaid bills was further exasperated by the company losing focus of their core business model. Instead of staying true to their philosophy, they abandoned their position in the underserved low-fare, no-frills market and rushed headlong into the already overcrowded full-service market. And, much like the prideful king who was intent on reaching just a little higher so he could be the first to touch the moon, People Express came tumbling down.

Setting Aside Our Egos

Now, contrast this story with that of Southwest Airlines. Unlike their competitors rapid and ultimately, destructive growth cycle, Southwest has expanded slowly and deliberately in the little more than four decades they have been in business. In fact, in their first four years in operation, they went from three aircraft and three cities to five aircraft and four cities. That is a mere fraction of the growth experienced by People Express in the same timeframe.

Additionally, they, unlike People Express, have stayed the course with their basic service model. That is, they've adapted their approach as circumstances dictate while avoiding the temptation to be all things to all people. The leaders at Southwest airlines understand their product may not be for everyone and are completely fine with that. They know their niche and have consistently exercised the self control to stick to their plan.

In a nutshell, Southwest Airlines has become the most successful passenger carrier in history by not falling prey to the allure of being the largest, or for that matter, even dominating any specific route. Instead, their enduring success stems from the fact that company leaders have always been careful to guard themselves from the pitfalls wrought of prideful ambition by maintaining the self control to stay focused on what the company and its leaders said mattered most—serving others. Their unwavering commitment to their employees, customers, and shareholders guarding them from succumbing to what one-time CEO Herb Kelleher shared was the primary reason he believes People Express ultimately failed: *Hubris*.

Parting Thoughts

Andrew Carnegie was one of the richest, most successful men of his generation. A Scottish immigrant of extremely humble beginnings, he co-founded the world's first billion dollar corporation, U.S. Steel. However, Carnegie never became prideful or arrogant. In fact, he is perhaps most famous for always attributing his success not to his innate skills, talents or work ethic but rather, to the talents of others. He always sought the best in those around them and in response, people consistently and willingly delivered. Perhaps it should be no surprise that this extremely self-controlled man chose this most modest of inscriptions for his tombstone: "Here lies a man who knew how to enlist the service of better men than himself."[165]

Committing to rejecting mediocrity and leading our lives in a more excellent way demands we never forget how our ego can serve as either friend or foe. On the one

WARNING

An unchecked ego can quickly get the better of us, distorting our perspective of who we are, what we are capable of, and of the role others play in both our success and failure

hand, it is our ego that puts steel in the spine and gives us the strength and vision to think differently, act boldly, and strive to become the best version of ourselves possible. However, we must also recognize how an unchecked ego can quickly get the better of us, distorting our perspective of who we are, what we are capable of, and of the role others play in both our success and failure. It is only when ego is properly tempered by self-control that we open ourselves to heeding the inner voice of wisdom and reason that whispers, "Hold on a minute. Why are you choosing to do this?" "Are you seeking to serve yourself, or are you doing what is best to serve the greater good?"[166]

How we chose to respond to this inner dialogue speaks volumes of our commitment to living up to the moral standards we expect of ourselves and want to see replicated in others.[167] The challenge for all of us in rejecting mediocrity as the norm in a "me-centric" society then is to remain ever vigilant of the hubris born of overconfidence. In a world where success is often measured in terms of what people can get, grab or gather for themselves, we have to *choose to exercise a different kind of leadership*. Specifically, we have to guard ourselves from becoming so focused on achieving excellence in our own lives that we fail to help others experience it in theirs, as well.

Sixth-century B.C. Chinese philosopher Lao-Tzu astutely pointed out that "at no time in the world will a man who is sane over reach himself, over-spend himself, over-rate himself." For those of us committed to being active participants in the process of positive change, we must consciously guard ourselves from ever becoming so enamored with our own ideas, talents, and success that we follow the same path as the self-absorbed and unregulated box-stacking king—tricking ourselves into building a pride-fueled tower to the moon that all but guarantees we too will eventually take a fall.

Chapter 16

Practice Thankfulness

Feeling gratitude and not expressing it is
like wrapping a present and not giving it.
—William Arthur Ward

In August 1914, an intrepid British explorer named Ernest Shackleton and his crew boarded the ship *Endurance*.[168] He and his team of twenty-seven men set sail for the South Atlantic, intent to be the first to cross Antarctica. However, in October 1915, still half a continent away from their intended destination, their ship was crushed by massive sheets of ice.

Drifting on ice packs, the crew's food and water quickly disappeared. But Shackleton and his men, resolved to consistently demonstrating a sense of mutual care and support to one another despite the harshness of their environment, forged on.

Shackleton, who was brilliant at building morale, cohesion, and cooperation, constantly reinforced to his men that they were one in this ordeal and would live or perish together. Intentionally looking for ways to lift his men's spirits as they struggled to survive amidst the extremely harsh conditions, he took every opportunity to express gratitude for even the smallest of triumphs. Willfully building value into his men's lives one kind word or encouraging gesture at a time.

More than a year after the shipwreck and struggling to stay alive, Shackleton and his men found themselves stranded on a very small island. With food dwindling and hope for rescue fading, Shackleton realized the only true chance of survival he and his team had was for someone to set out in an open boat across the stormiest ocean on the globe to try and reach a small settlement some 800 miles away.

It was a seemingly impossible task in one of the worlds most dangerous, unforgiving and far-away places.

Recognizing, and more importantly, accepting, that it was his responsibility to lead the change he wanted to see in his surroundings, he solicited five volunteers to accompany him and together, they set sail in pursuit of this final outpost of hope.

As things would have it, it was a chance which ultimately paid off. The group successfully reached their destination and marshaled help for their still stranded teammates. And in the end, against all odds, everyone survived. Everyone! Not a single person was lost despite finding themselves stranded in a harsh, turbulent and frightening place—a half a world away from home.

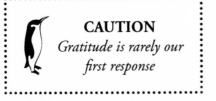

CAUTION
Gratitude is rarely our first response

A century later, many people still speak or write about Shackleton's incredible story of survival and marvel at his incredible persistence. His relentless desire to continue forward despite the seemingly insurmountable odds he faced inspires each of us to think about how we would conduct ourselves should we encounter similar challenging circumstances. But in my view, one of the most important lessons to be learned from this amazing story is how it was largely Shackleton's deep-seated sense of gratefulness and appreciation for life's simplest blessings that infused him and his men with the strength to forge forward when conditions were bleakest. Through his words and his ways he understood how possessing an attitude of gratitude is essential if we are to flourish and thrive, both in good times and bad.

An Attitude of Gratitude

We all likely know at least one amazing person who, no matter what trauma or tragedy he or she may encounter, maintains a contagious optimism. As the incredible story of Earnest Shackleton affirms, being exposed to such strength of character and graciousness, even in the midst of life's greatest storms, leaves us feeling encouraged and inspired. Their positive example and attitude of gratitude infuses us with energy to keep moving forward when it would be far easier to accept mediocrity as the norm.

Gratitude has been defined as possessing or experiencing a sense of thankfulness in response to receiving something beneficial. Webster's dictionary describes it as "the quality of feeling or being grateful or thankful." In many ways, it is the ultimate positive emotion as it expands our sense of well-being and enhances our appreciation toward those people or things that brighten our day or lighten our load. Perhaps this is why gratitude is frequently described as *a gift that keeps on giving.*[169]

Despite being touted for thousands of years by a host of religions and philosophies as an integral component of health, wholeness, and well-being, gratitude largely remained a "forgotten factor" in psychological and sociological research.

Until recently, that is.

With the advent of the science of Positive Psychology, numerous researchers and scientists have shown how gratefulness is a particularly powerful transformative practice. Acting as an emotional reset switch of sorts, gratitude equips us to completely change our outlook about life; willfully directing our thoughts to the positive aspects of our existence.

Leading the charge to explain the numerous benefits wrought of routinely employing an attitude of gratitude are psychologists Robert Emmons of U.C. Davis and Michael McCullough of the University of Miami. Together, they've repeatedly found that practicing gratitude can put us on a path to flourishing and thriving, elevating not only our performance, but improving the lives of those around us in the process. In fact, their ongoing Research Project on Gratitude and Thankfulness has repeatedly found that people who choose to proactively do something to make gratefulness a regular habit, such as keeping a weekly gratitude journal or reflecting on what one has to be thankful for before going to sleep at night, experience fewer physical ailments, exercise more, and are more likely to reach their personal and professional goals and aspirations.

One of the primary reasons this invisible process of reflecting on all the reasons we currently have to feel thankful works so well is because it triggers a physiological reaction within us. In addition to setting into motion a series of positive emotions which leave us feeling more alert, alive, interested, and enthusiastic than before, it provides us the confidence to risk stepping out in new directions.[170] And if that were not benefit enough, gratitude also serves as a proven stress buffer as it makes us less likely to experience envy, anger, resentment, regret, fear, and the many other unpleasant states of mind that keep us paralyzed in place; unwitting accomplices of a mediocre me mindset.[171]

Transforming Gratefulness into Action

Many leaders are unable to pinpoint the exact moment they've been so dramatically struck by a clear realization of just how grateful they were for the simple blessings in their lives. Simone Honikman, however, remembers with great clarity the day she was jolted into realizing just how fortunate she was.

A doctor in Cape Town, South Africa, her first daughter had just turned one year old when she attended a conference on maternal mental health. It was 2002, and following decades of segregation, the country was just starting to stand on its own two feet.

Although originally compelled to attend the conference because it offered an impressive array of presenters from around the world, Simone remembers being shocked to learn of the extraordinarily high rate of postnatal depression occurring in the outskirts of her city. Not more than a dozen miles from her home, she was heartbroken to hear that a staggering 35 percent of mothers in the impoverished suburbs of Cape Town were experiencing a paralyzing sense of hopelessness at a rate nearly three times higher than developed countries. "I was so struck," she recalls, "by the paradoxes of pain and motherhood—of deprivation and affluence. I felt compelled to do something…Not doing anything would have been intolerable."[172]

Admittedly, at the time Simone was struck by the realization so many in her immediate surroundings were in dire need of assistance, she also became intensely aware of how truly blessed she was. She enjoyed great health, a loving family, a new baby, the opportunity to go to school and study her passion, medicine; and now enjoyed the privilege of putting that passion into practice each day in a multitude of ways. As her sense of gratefulness swelled, she found her willingness to reach out and do something to build value into her surroundings grew in proportion.

Within weeks of attending the conference she chose to establish the Postnatal Mental Health Project (PMHP). Receiving early support from the midwives and administrators of the hospital in which she worked, she began providing free screening for women, mostly from low-income communities. She quickly expanded into counseling and psychological services for new, primarily poor, single mothers. And her innovative approach began to pay off almost immediately.[173]

Take the story of Gloria from Cape Town, for instance. Pregnant at fourteen and worried about how she would support herself at such a young age, she suffered her first severe depression. She went on to suffer through two more depressions in later pregnancies, until she finally found PMHP. The services she received helped stabilize her situation, transforming her sense of powerlessness into a positive attitude about motherhood that equipped her to better care for her children.

Then there is Babalwe, a shy, young woman with a history of verbal and physical abuse at the hands of family members. Pregnant as a teenager and suicidal, Babalwe's depression made it difficult for her to work to support herself—until she started receiving free counseling from PMHP. Within months of visiting the clinic, and with a new-found hope in her heart, she boldly set out to create a better life for herself.

And she hasn't looked back since.

Today, more than thirteen thousand women and scores of children in South Africa have benefitted from PMHP's actions since its founding almost a decade ago.[174] Their ability to rewrite the story lines of their lives can be traced back to a single leader, Simone Honikman. A force for good in her surroundings whose renewed sense of thankfulness for the many blessings she enjoyed in her life encouraged her to generously practice gratefulness in her own backyard.[175]

Cultivating a Heart of Gratitude

I love the story of the young man with the bandaged hand who approached the clerk at the post office. "Sir, could you please address this post card for me?" The clerk, happy to help, agreed to write the message on the card.

Once complete, the postal clerk asked the young man if there was anything else he could do for him. The young man looked at the card and then said, "Yes. Would you please add a P.S., Please excuse the handwriting."

As this tongue-in-cheek tale illuminates, gratitude is rarely our first response. For all the benefits of gratefulness, it's just not a virtue we naturally put into practice. So why is it so few of us follow Ernest Shackleton's and Simone Honikman's inspiring example and make counting and expressing our blessings more of a driving force for positive change in our surroundings? Psychologists tell us there are a host of reasons why this is so. The most notable being the flawed sense some of us possess that accepting other peoples varied forms of unsolicited kindness marks us as a passive victim. Other reasons why gratitude is routinely blocked is an unhealthy preoccupation with materialism and a lack of self-awareness and self reflection.

Of course, you may notice that almost every one of these hindrances to gratitude revolve around one primary theme—too much focus on ourselves. When we possess an unhealthy and inflated sense of our own importance, we erroneously believe we are deserving of special attention, rights, or privileges. All of which lead us to expect or demand special favors without assuming reciprocal responsibilities.

One of the most effective ways we can learn to be more grateful, both for what we have and for those who make our own success possible, is to get into the practice of counting our blessings

CAUTION
For all the benefits of gratefulness, it's just not a virtue we naturally put into practice

and then committing to being a blessing, ourselves. Martin Seligman, one of the cofounders of Positive Psychology and today a researcher and Professor at the University of Pennsylvania, has made it a top priority in his work to prove just how powerful reflecting and then enacting gratefulness can be, both individually and collectively.[176]

In one popular study, Seligman chose to ask his students to document their blessings. Specifically, he asked them to write down five things for which they felt grateful for, once a week, for 10 weeks in a row. The results were eye-opening, with students reporting feeling less stressed, more content, optimistic and satisfied with their lives. Simply by taking a couple minutes every week to think about and document those things, big and small, they were most thankful for in the moment.

Even more interesting, however, is what happened when Dr. Seligman asked his student to write gratitude *letters* to individuals and then conduct gratitude *visits* in order to read those letters aloud to the recipient. In virtually every instance, feelings of mutual appreciation increased and both parties reported deriving a deeper sense of pleasure and satisfaction from the relationship.

What this tells us is it that, although counting our blessings on a regular basis can certainly improve our mood and elevates our overall level of health and happiness, making it a priority to *express* genuine thankfulness to others will do so even more. The question now is simply, how? The answer, fortunately, is equally straightforward. Choose to frequently put into play two of the most profoundly powerful words in the world...*thank you.*

The Simplest Way to Express Gratitude

Renowned humanitarian, philosopher, and theologian Albert Schweitzer once wrote, "to educate yourself for the feeling of gratitude means to take nothing for granted...Train yourself never to put off the word or action for the expression of gratitude."

As the above quote expresses, we can never go wrong communicating our gratefulness to others in word or deed. So with this perspective as a backdrop, let me ask you another question. Every day consists of 86,400 seconds. How many of them have you used today to say "thank you?"

"Thank You" is a universally recognized phrase that transcends culture, race, tradition, gender, status, language, and age. The power of simply expressing thanks is proven to motivate, validate, and give positive reinforcement. Be it in your home, workplace, worship space, community, it can even do wonders to elevate moods, enhance relationships, or as Ernest Shackleton and Simone Honikman teach us, it can even help keep hope afloat when things are looking particularly grim in our surroundings.[177]

But, for all the power of your words, it turns out that one of the most powerful ways to express gratitude to others is to go old school with your thanks. That is, in this era of emails and texts, Facebook and Twitter, the simple act of writing a handwritten expression of gratitude can go a very long way to communicating your genuine commitment to leading your life in a more excellent way.

One of the primary reasons a written thank you works is that it has lasting value. It can be read, reread, and shared with family or friends. While a verbal comment can often express the same sentiments, a handwritten thank you touches us in ways that are proven to make us want to reciprocate. So much, in fact, that in a study of consumer tipping behavior, researchers found that servers who simply added a handwritten "thank you" to the restaurant bill elicited about 11 percent higher tips than those who did not.[178]

The value of frequently expressing thanks, however, isn't just good for your health. It's also great for your business. Study after study reveals that company's whose employees routinely say "Thank you" to their customers benefit from both improved revenue and increased referrals. Plus, scores of industrial psychologists and organizational performance consultants chronicle how employee productivity, retention, morale, innovation, and commitment skyrocket when leaders make it a priority to express appreciation to workmates on a regular basis.

A host of renowned bosses are quick to point out the importance of thanking people, including the late

NOTE

The most powerful ways to express gratitude to others is to go old school with your thanks

Robert Townsend, former CEO of Avis. In his book, *Up the Organization*, he recounts how sharing a simple "Thanks" is a really neglected form of compensation. Max DePree, author of the classic *Leadership is an Art* and former CEO of furniture giant Herman Miller, described saying "thank you" as among a leader's primary responsibilities. And Doug Conant, the former CEO of Campbell Soup who hand wrote over 30,000 thank you notes to his employees during his tenure, believed it was this simple act of expressed gratitude which did more than anything else to energize his once ailing company to attain (and maintain, I'd add) the success Campbell Soup company continues to enjoy today.

So, with all this said, remember, gratitude is like a muscle. The more we do with it the stronger it gets. In the words of Meister Eckert, "If the only prayer you said in your whole life was, "thank you," that would suffice." I'd add that's quite a return-on-investment just for sharing two single syllable words that don't cost you anything to use, anyway.

Parting Thoughts

The philosopher Cicero once said, "Gratitude is not only the greatest of virtues but the parent of all the others."[179] Years later, sociologist Georg Simmel referred to gratitude as "the moral memory of mankind…if every grateful action…were suddenly eliminated, society (at least as we know it) would break apart."[180]

What these insightful words alert us to is how routinely expressing grateful thoughts and actions towards others makes us more willing to accept responsibility for others, less likely to judge the value of others based on their position or possessions, and more conscientious, more agreeable, more compassionate, and less envious and egotistical than non grateful people. In other words, it positions us to reflect humanity operating at its peak, positive capacity.

But what's essential to recognize is that, although we all have opportunities to express thankfulness, too few of us *choose* to regularly act on those opportunities. One but need to look at the low levels of employee engagement in our workplaces, assess the number of discouraged children and spouses in our homes, or examine the difficulties we seem to have to building and sustaining mutually beneficial relationships in our communities to see gratitude, though in abundant supply, is a commodity many fail to frequently share.

British writer G. K. Chesterton, considered by many one of the major literary figures of the 20th century, produced almost 100 books in his lifetime. Covering a wide-array of fields such as faith, philosophy, biography, poetry, mystery, and even social and political commentary, his influence on literature was eclipsed only by his zeal for life. To what was this sense of ever-present exuberance and exhilaration attributed? In a word, it was *gratitude*.

In his autobiography, written just before his passing in 1936, Chesterton summarized his view of gratitude as "if not the doctrine I have always taught, is the doctrine I should have always liked to teach."[181] Today, almost eight decades after he wrote those words, their meaning rings ever true. That is, they remain a testimony to the truth that there exists no lack of opportunities to practice gratefulness in and through our lives, only an absence of commitment. Only we can choose to see the gifts of a kind word, pleasant note of thanks, or simple, affirming touch as something worth sharing. But first, we have to willfully overcome our propensity to take things for granted, to feel entitled, or to become so caught up pursuing our own agendas that we fail to notice the beauty present right before our eyes.

Remember, every moment is spring loaded with possibilities to make our world a better, brighter places to live, work, play, and pray. We simply need to remain aware that in order to expect blessings we must resolve to first be a blessing.[182]

Why not choose to start today?

The Final Choice

MAKE YOUR
CHARACTER COUNT...
BE REAL

*It does not take a majority to prevail...but rather an irate, tireless
minority, keen on setting brushfires of freedom in the minds of men.*
—Samuel Adams

Chapter 17

Character: Coin
of the Realm

*Character, in the long run, is the decisive factor
in the life of an individual and of nations alike.*
—Theodore Roosevelt

For most of us, Raoul Wallenberg is not a familiar name. This is unfortunate, as this Swedish diplomat's selfless, courageous actions in Budapest, Hungary, during World War II are credited with having saved well over one hundred thousand lives.[183] His story, though not well known, epitomizes what it means to lead life in a more excellent way.

During the waning months of World War II, the United States and her allies were desperate to find a way to slow or stop Nazi Germany's merciless slaughter of millions of innocent Jewish civilians in Eastern Europe. Despite the prospects of victory dimming by the day, the Nazi war machine became ever more determined to complete their "final solution" by making extermination of the Jews a foremost priority.[184]

With the death camps operating at near maximum capacity, the Allied powers felt powerless to do anything to stop the genocide. But quite unexpectedly, an unlikely leader materialized in the form of a young, wealthy, upper-class Swede from a well-connected, prominent family.

Raoul Wallenberg was age thirty-two when a friend approached him to inquire if he would be willing to intercede on the Jewish people's behalf.[185] In addition to not being Jewish himself, the heir-apparent to the vast Wallenberg financial empire had nothing to gain and everything to lose by accepting this formidable challenge. Yet, when asked if he would consider doing something to help change the situation, he jumped at the opportunity.

Adopting the cover of a Swedish diplomat, Wallenberg quickly devised a plan to create false Swedish passports that he could distribute to potential victims as a means of providing them safe passage out of Nazi-controlled territory. At the same time, he quickly got to work establishing a series of safe houses within Hungary under the guise of Swedish government buildings. This, he believed, would provide the inhabitants diplomatic immunity.

Within weeks of his arrival, Wallenberg and a series of contacts he cultivated distributed over twenty thousand forged Swedish passports to Hungarian Jews. They led another thirteen thousand to refuge in the "diplomatic" safe houses.[186]

But he knew still much more needed to be done.

Saving a Nation

Shortly after Wallenberg's arrival, the Germans were forced to divert the trains carrying the Hungarian civilians to the death camps so they could be used to help move supplies to support their burgeoning war effort. But this did not stop or even slow the enemy's desire to destroy the helpless Jewish citizens. In fact, it made them all the crueler, now forcing people to walk the 125 miles to their own destruction. But all this sordid twist did was make young Wallenberg all the bolder in doing what he could, when we could, where he could, to try and save the Jewish people.

Historical accounts document how on numerous occasions, Wallenberg would arrive at the few stopping areas between the villages and the Nazi death camps, pockets bulging with passports and Red Cross trucks in tow. Paying little heed to the Nazi guards, who quite honestly did not know how to handle this confident young diplomat who courageously waded into the crowd to identify and save "Swedish citizens," Wallenberg never hesitated in giving his best for the benefit of those around him. And on more than one occasion, it was said he would simply whisper to those he had to leave behind, "I am sorry. I am trying to take the youngest ones first," he explained. "I want to save a nation."[187]

Time and time again, Wallenberg and his team would intercept a death march and begin handing out newly minted passports, quickly whisking away another group of prisoners to safety. But what one eyewitness remembers as most extraordinary about Wallenberg "was the absolutely convincing power of *his behavior*."[188]

Leadership: You Know It When You See It

Although few Jewish people ever even saw Wallenberg's face, everyone was talking about his selfless, courageous actions. Inspiring hope and a bias for action in many of those who otherwise felt powerless to affect their circumstances, he became an incredible force for good in a part of the world dominated primarily by despair—a shining example of the virtue that often lies hidden within each and every human spirit.[189]

> **NOTE**
> *Although leadership can often be challenging to define, you certainly know it when you see it*

On many occasions, alone and in the middle of enemy territory, Wallenberg produced one miracle after another. His willingness to take risks, exercise physical and moral courage, and demonstrate unwavering self-confidence simply dumbfounded his adversaries. In the words of Wallenberg profilers John Kunich and Richard Lester, "Here was someone thickly cloaked in apparent authority, but utterly devoid of actual political or military power. Here was a man who was everything they [the enemy] wished they could be in terms of personal strength of character, but for the fact that he was their polar opposite in purpose."[190]

When peace finally came to Europe in 1945, Wallenberg's fate took a very different turn. He simply vanished, never to be seen or heard from again. He left only a lasting memory of a man who was intent to lead his life in a more excellent way. A leader through and though whose example helps us better understand that although leadership can often be challenging to define, *you certainly know it when you see it.*[191]

Today in Israel, a grove of trees known as the Avenue of the Righteous memorializes those who risked their lives to help Jews during the Holocaust. Along with Raoul Wallenberg's tree, there is a medal inscribed in the language of the Jewish Talmud that summarizes his memory in the words, "Whoever saves a single soul, it is as if he had saved the whole world."[192]

Wallenberg had the choice to live a life of luxury, far from the pain and suffering of what was occurring in Hungary. Yet he chose to reject mediocrity and walk differently in the world. Willingly deviating from what was comfortable and safe, he chose to be part of the solution in one of history's most devastating moments. Not for fame or glory, but to serve humanity in their greatest time of need.

In the words of Gideon Hausner, "In this age where there is so little to believe in—so very little on which our young people can pin their hopes and ideals—he is a person to *show* to the world, which knows so little about him. That is why I believe the story of Raoul Wallenberg should be told and his figure, in all its proportions, projected into the human minds."[193]

I certainly could not agree more.

Character: The Coin of the Realm

Examples of leaders like Raoul Wallenberg who courageously choose to think differently, act boldly, and be the best version of themselves by selflessly serving others provides us with living, breathing definitions of *character*. And although we use this word frequently, we rarely take the time to fully unpack and understand it, despite its almost unquantifiable significance to us as human beings.

The word *character* derives from a Greek word that means "to mark," which originates from the centuries-old practice of engraving the likeness of important figures on metal coins. Be it emperors, kings, or heroes, the appearance of a distinctive, difficult-to-forge caricature on silver or some other form of precious metal was designed to build trust and facilitate mutually beneficial transactions between people.

Character continues to do the same for us today.

Study after study continues to validate the premium we place on character. In research involving twenty-five thousand leaders rated by more than two hundred thousand evaluators, character was identified as the quintessential quality that distinguishes great performers from the rest of the pack.[194] Similarly, an independent study conducted by the Corporate Leadership Council found that team members identified character as the most desirable attribute for both coworkers and supervisors alike.[195]

In a world where it's all too easy to fall prey to the fleeting promises of various fads and whims, the leaders most people want to follow are those like Raoul Wallenberg. Individuals whose examples remind us we are at our best not when we are solely intent satisfying our own agendas, but rather, when we are willing to give the best of ourselves in service to something larger than ourselves—one opportunity at a time.

The Character Ethic

Dr. Stephen Covey made a remarkable discovery during his landmark research into American success literature written between 1776 and 1976. Specifically, he found that in the first one hundred fifty years of our nation's history, the literature emphasized the development of character and ability as the sure path to success. Covey labeled this approach *the character ethic.*

In contrast, the subsequent fifty years of success literature focused heavily on the use and development of surface-level personality skills and techniques to portray a successful image—whether or not the image coincided with underlying reality. Covey termed this *the personality ethic.*

In most recent times, he noted that this societal focus on image and personality has become even more pronounced. In a world where superficiality is sufficient and cosmetic self-improvement is celebrated, the personality ethic is preferred.

And why not?

After all, it's easier to focus on making an impression than it is to do the hard work of building your character.

Ultimately, however, success as a leader can only truly occur if we are securely anchored to the reality of who we are, inside and out. Which means it takes real commitment and hard work. As Jedd Medefind and Erik Lokkesmoe affirm, while "impression settles for a quick coat of cheerful paint; the character builder repairs dry rot with lumber, nails, and sweat. Impression seeks a slim waist using diet pills and a cinched-up corset; the character builder relies on exercise and vegetables."[196]

Hence, a mediocre me mindset convinces us to be satisfied accepting superficiality over substance; convenience over conviction; and ease over excellence. None of which, I remind you, set us on a path to grow one step closer to becoming the very best version of ourselves possible.

Unfortunately, examples of people who make it into the limelight only to subsequently neglect their character abound. And although their skill in projecting a particular persona may propel them to the top for a season, only a leader with character can be counted on to stay there for the duration. As leadership author and expert Tim Elmore likes to say, "If you don't have strong character, you will eventually sabotage your leadership."[197]

We've seen this sad truth play out repeatedly across society in the last couple of decades, witnessing everyone from televangelists, politicians, businessmen, military officers, and even a president fall victim to immorality, fraud, and scandal. But it surely didn't start with this generation. Failures in character litter the landscape of history, leaving some of our world's most tragic memories in their wake.

> **NOTE**
> *We are at our best not when we are simply serving ourselves or satisfying our agendas, but rather when we are giving the best of ourselves in service to something larger than ourselves*

For example, one hundred years ago a boy named Schicklegruber grew up in Europe. As a teen, he never heard about the importance of character. His parents never took the time to teach him the difference between right and wrong, and he began to develop his own ideals. His father put him down when he talked about becoming a priest and ridiculed him at the thought of his pursuing his passion for art. He was never told he was valued, nor was he ever taught values. One night he overheard his parents arguing about moving away, and he became convinced they didn't love him and would leave him behind.

So he ran away.

This discouraged and desperate little boy became a man. The man became a leader. You know him as Adolph Hitler. The very same man who set out to eliminate the Jewish population in World War II that Raoul Wallenberg gave his life to try and save.

Although Hitler certainly possessed leadership *skills,* he lacked what mattered most to put those skills to good use: *character.*[198] His sordid example serving as a lasting testimony that true leadership, the kind that will compel people to do what they can, when they can, where they can to lead their lives in a more excellent way, is built from the inside out. The visible is only a reflection of the invisible, but the invisible is, ultimately, what matters most.

Parting Thoughts

It's interesting to note how Napoleon and Washington were both great statesmen and accomplished military leaders. But what a difference in their character! One was a ruthless conqueror, building a glittering and evanescent empire on an ocean of blood, dying in exile on a lonely island, and leaving behind a legacy of pain, sorrow, and selfishness. Washington, on the other hand, refused a crown. Instead of turning the spotlight of attention to himself, he selflessly chose to bend the light toward what he believed mattered most: serving the legitimate needs of others. And as a result, he used his influence to help lay the foundation for a nation destined to be infinitely greater than Napoleon's empire ever was.

Two men, both leaders, chose to lead very different lives. One lived for the here and now. Intent to get and grab as much as he could for himself, leading was a means to fulfill his desire for personal power, fame, and glory.

The other chose to exercise the strength of character to think differently, act boldly, and be the best version of himself in order to serve a purpose greater than himself.

Pause and ask yourself which one of these best describes you?

In closing, I'd ask you to recall the earlier metaphor of the powerful elephant paralyzed in place by the power of the status-quo bias? The fact of the matter is, he already possesses all the strength he needs to break free. His liberty isn't hampered by his potential; it's hindered by his fear of stepping out in a new and uncertain direction.

The reason I like the metaphor of the elephant so much is that it reminds us liberty is first and foremost a matter of perception. We are all free to think and do as we please. The limitation isn't in our capabilities; it's mainly in where we, as individuals, *choose* to draw our personal lines of responsibility around what we value. If we want to break the cycle of mediocrity that exists in so many segments of our society today, especially as it relates to our roles as leaders, we have to be willing to make the first move: rejecting passivity, embracing responsibility, and committing to leading positively.

Anne Frank once said, "How wonderful it is that nobody need wait a single moment before starting to improve the world." Despite the horrors she and her family experienced during World War II, she identified the power we each possess to *choose* to make good things happen.

Yet another reminder we are each already as much of a leader as we choose to be.

Chapter 18

Don't Chunk!

*Be more concerned with your character than your
reputation, because your character is what you really are,
while your reputation is merely what others think you are.*
—John Wooden

G o to any military base and you will undoubtedly encounter
a robust security system. The most visible elements are the
well-constructed fence and continuously manned front gate.
However, you'll also likely come across a series of stubby but very
sturdy concrete posts called bollards, designed to provide separation and
protection of both facilities and personnel.

Now imagine that you are given the difficult job of removing one of
these posts with a sledgehammer. I say difficult because they are usually
several feet high, a half a foot thick, and solid concrete. It's a strong,
sturdy, and rigid structure designed to withstand many blows.

So you begin the task at hand by swinging the sledgehammer with all
you've got. Boom! But little changes after delivering your blow. At best,
the post suffers one small chunk for all the effort expended.

Committed to the task at hand, you swing the hammer again and again, and every time, one little chunk is all that falls away from the post. At this rate, you think, it will take forever to finish this job.

But although the external damage seems negligible, what you can't see is what's happening internally. In actuality, with every blow, the internal structure of the concrete post is becoming weaker and weaker. Although you can only see superficial change on the outside, the real damage is being done on the inside.

Boom! Chunk.

Boom! Chunk.

On and on you go, and before you know it, that once formidable strong, sturdy, and rigid concrete structure has been reduced to a pile of dust.

What's the point? Namely, our character is much like that concrete post. It too is formidable. But life is also full of sledgehammers.[199] Every time we fall into the trap of accepting mediocrity and sticking with the status quo because it's safer, easier, or more comfortable than doing what we know must be done to promote positive change in our surroundings, we risk the hammer. When we fail to be true to ourselves, acting in ways that violate our values, we deliver another invisible blow to our character that, in time, can reduce our lives to a pile of rubble.

Character Builds Strength: Individually and Collectively

Being a leader of character means we must be willing to demonstrate firsthand that we want our lives to count for something important. The possibility that we can help create better, brighter, healthier surroundings, however, will not materialize by accident. It will take leadership. Not just any kind of leadership, but responsible leadership committed to making the development of character a lifelong priority.

The positive effects of intentionally developing character were recently reinforced in a study of twenty different schools across the state of Hawaii. The research effort, designed to promote a school-wide transformation, included all ages from kindergarten through twelfth grade.[200]

The key element of the study involved emphasizing activities to build character that go beyond traditional rules or policies to control or punish problem behaviors. The purpose was to create an enhanced sense of *responsible self-leadership* grounded in the commitment to always conduct oneself in a manner that communicates respect for others and seeks continual individual and collective improvement. The impressive results of the initiative speak for itself.

NOTE

The sooner we make character development a priority in our lives, the better equipped we will be to operate at peak capacity

At the end of the intentional character-building effort, researchers determined that overall school quality climbed 21 percent; suspensions plummeted 72 percent; absenteeism declined 15 percent; and dramatic increases in reading and math skills were achieved as well.[201] Commenting on the positive nature of the findings, an Ohio State University professor in the School of Social and Behavioral Health Sciences explained that the effort validated how improving social and character skills leaves more room for teachers to teach and students to learn and be more motivated. He added, "What we're finding now is that we can really address some of the concerns in our schools by focusing more on character in the classroom."[202]

As this latest in a series of reports confirms, the sooner we make character development a priority in our lives, the better equipped we will be to operate at peak performance. So how can we continue to develop our character, you ask? I'd offer we do so by routinely putting into practice the countercultural attitudes and actions we've been exploring in this book. Choosing to demonstrate by our words and our ways that we are unafraid to say no to the status quo and yes to leading our lives in a more excellent way—one opportunity to build value into our surroundings at a time.

A Compelling Call for a New, Unconventional Type of Leader

There is a famous story of a nobleman, Sir Philip Sidney, who, fighting for his beloved England in the sixteenth century, was mortally wounded on the battlefield. Though he was desperately thirsty from loss of blood, he chose to do the unexpected and gave away his water flask to a dying young soldier. His final words, "Thy necessity is yet greater than mine," serve as a stark contrast to how the majority of people of power, privilege, and position of his era would have likely acted in that moment, had they found themselves facing the same choice.

As I said at the outset of our journey together, different is good. In fact, it can be very, very good. Throughout these pages I've shared with you example after example of leaders who have chosen to be different. Like Sir Philip Sidney, their unconventional attitudes and counterintuitive actions get our attention. Their willingness to deviate from established norms in order to make a stand for what they believe is worth fighting for providing a countercultural example worth emulating.

In this vein, I remember when former Secretary of Defense Robert Gates stood in front of a crowd of current and future military leaders at the United States military's Air War College in 2008 and delivered an unexpected, if not somewhat startling, call to unconventional action. In his words that crisp spring morning, he made it abundantly clear that the kind of people our nation and our world need to guide us through these uncertain times are "...creative, reform-minded leaders." Men and women who possess the entrepreneurial spirit to overcome their fears and think and act "outside the box" so they can help develop creative, relevant solutions to our most prevalent and persistent problems.[203]

But that's not all he said.

The former Secretary, known for his candor and his willingness to deviate from the status quo himself, went on to cite the example of the late US Air Force Colonel John Boyd, a leader Gates affectionately termed a "maverick." Boyd, a notoriously independent thinker renowned for marching to the beat of a very different drummer, was an amazing innovator whose bold ideas have been adopted by businesses and organizations across the globe.[204] But, like other unconventional leaders throughout history, Boyd was eventually asked to leave the military. His staunch personal preference for doing "something" rather than simply settling with being "somebody" proved more important to him than anything else.[205]

The fact that the Secretary of Defense would choose the example of someone who was forced out of uniform because he was viewed as too unconventional speaks volumes. Michael Wyly, a now-retired army colonel, summarizes the significance of this most unlikely of leadership speeches by Secretary Gates in an article appropriately titled "In Praise of Mavericks." "For a defense secretary to quote a maverick colonel who left the Air Force as a pariah was a bold and risky step…But perhaps the most unfortunate thing is that we have to think of him as a maverick. *He should have been the norm.*"[206]

Colonel John Boyd, the man who was largely responsible for the development and design of several of our nation's most effective fighter programs, whose ideas transformed the way America fights its wars, and whose theories on how to effectively cope with uncertainty continue to be taught across the military, academia, and the business community, was an unconventional thinker without parallel.[207] He was someone who understood that one day, each of us will face a fork in the road. If we choose to go the road most traveled, to follow what the majority are doing, we have a strong chance of "being somebody." This will make us members of the club of common people choosing a common path. Or, in Secretary Gates' own words, "You can go [the other] way and you can [choose] to do something—something for your country and for…yourself."[208]

This, however, isn't just a choice for those who wear the uniform. It's a choice we all have to make ourselves, each and every day.

Choose to be different and lead the change we want to see in our surroundings? Or sit on the sidelines and watch others do all the work of making the world a better, brighter place? Whatever your choice, know this: how you respond speaks volumes of your willingness to either be part of the solution to our nation's most perplexing problems, or to remain part of the problem.

There can be no more fence sitting.

Breaking the Rules

John Boyd chose to lead his life by different rules. His countercultural example demonstrating how revolting against business-as-usual is sometimes required if truly want to raise the bar on our performance.

But don't just take my word for it. .

In their best-selling book, *First, Break All the Rules: What the World's Greatest Managers Do Differently,* Gallup organization consultants Marcus Buckingham and Curt Coffman share how twenty-five years of exhaustive research, which included over eighty-thousand interviews, found that the most successful leaders they studied were those who chose to routinely "break the rules and make ones that work."[209] Their commitment to thinking more broadly about their role in the world empowers them to deviate from existing norms in pursuit of a purpose bigger than themselves.

Take Rosa Parks, for example.

It is unlikely Rosa Parks woke up one day and decided she suddenly needed to deviate from the beaten path and non-conform. But when the moment arose on that bus in Montgomery, Alabama, in 1955, she chose to step up instead of back down. Refusing to give up her seat and allow the shameful blight of segregation to continue unimpeded and unchallenged, she stayed true to her values, acting on her conviction that someone had to make a stand against the prevailing social system of the day.

And it might as well be her.

Yet Rosa Parks did something more than merely take a stand that day. You see, the courageous actions of this unassuming woman set into motion the wheels of the civil rights movement that netted a Supreme Court ruling less than a year later that rendered segregation on transportation unconstitutional.[210] Providing us with yet another example of how a single leader willing to think differently, act boldly, and be the best version of themselves possible can positively influence others to consider reaching higher, stretching further, and going farther than anyone would imagine is possible.

Parting Thoughts

One of the biggest questions before each of us today is, "What kind of America do we want?" The answer depends on how resolved each of us is to being part of the solution to society's most perplexing problems. As William Jennings Bryan once said, "Destiny is not a matter of chance; it is a matter of choice. It is not a thing to be waited for; it is a thing to be achieved."[211]

At a time when we need more leaders with the strength of character not to be merely observers in life, but to be active participants in the process of positive change, it's time to make a choice. Shrink back and accept that the mess we're currently in as good as it gets, or step up and do something to set a countercultural example worth emulating? Even if it means you have to break the rules and make new ones that work in the process.

Not long ago I came across a poem by ethicist and author Michael Josephson that speaks to what a life well lived looks like. I'd like to share it with you as I close out this chapter:

What will it matter?
Ready or not, some day it will all come to an end.
There will be no more sunrises, or minutes, hours, or days.
All the things you collected, whether treasured or forgotten will pass to someone else.
Your wealth, fame, and temporal power will shrivel to irrelevance.
It will not matter what you owned or what you were owed.
Your grudges, resentments, frustrations, and jealousies will finally disappear.
So too, your hopes, ambitions, plans, and to-do lists will expire.
The wins and losses that once seemed so important will fade away.
It won't matter where you came from or what side of the tracks you lived on at the end.
It won't even matter if you were beautiful or brilliant.
Even your gender and skin color will be irrelevant.
So what will matter? How will the value of your days be measured?
What will matter is not what you bought but what you built,
Not what you got but what you gave.
What will matter is not your success but your significance.
What will matter is not what you learned but what you taught.
What will matter is every act of integrity, compassion, courage, or sacrifice that enriched, empowered, or encouraged others to emulate your example.
What will matter is not your competence but your character.

What will matter is not how many people you knew, but how many will feel a lasting loss when you're gone.

What will matter is not your memories, but the memories that live on in those who loved you.

What will matter is not how long you will be remembered, but by whom and for what.

Living a life that matters doesn't happen by accident.

It's not a matter of circumstances but of choice.

Choose to live a life that matters.[212]

Remember, whatever choice you make speaks volume about your character…and reveals to an ever-watching world what you believe is truly worth fighting for in your life.

Choose wisely.

Conclusion

Lead Your Life
for a Higher Purpose

*"Leadership is the art of inspiring people to enthusiastically t
ake action toward achievement of uncommon goals."*
—Colonel John Boyd, USAF

What makes a young eighteen-year-old woman, former class president, and homecoming queen forgo college, lose all but a handful of her friends, and leave the comfort of her home and upscale lifestyle in Atlanta, Georgia, to move to Uganda, Africa, to become the adoptive mother of fourteen little girls, some with special needs? In simplest terms, it's transforming the desire to lead your life in a more excellent way into tangible action—something Katie Davis has wholeheartedly chosen to do. For the last five years, she has selflessly served as nurse, cook, employer, teacher, and friend to thousands of the planet's poorest people half a world away. It certainly wasn't something she had planned to do or was expected to do, mind you. But after taking a three-week mission trip as a high school senior, the direction of her life changed forever.

Within days of arriving in Uganda, Katie fondly recalls how she found herself moved by the men, women, and children of this country of thirty-three million people. Of which, over 50 percent of the population are under the age of fourteen, including two million orphans and scores of children as young as five who are serving as the head of their households.

When it was time to return home to friends and family in Atlanta following her visit, she did so largely with a heavy heart. Something had changed within her during this brief stay. When she arrived back in the States to finish her senior year, all she could think about was returning to the people in the small African nation that had captured her imagination and moved her to want to do something to lead the positive change she so desperately wanted to see occur in their lives.

By the time graduation arrived, Katie knew she had to go back. So, after a tearful goodbye to family, friends, boyfriend, and a sporty convertible, she boarded a plane for what she thought was going to be a ten-month commitment. But today, several years later, it's clear she has chosen to quit her life as she knew it for good.[213]

Shortly after her return to Africa, Katie found herself adopting a homeless orphan girl. She has since gone on to adopt thirteen other children, build a school, and develop a program that feeds 1,600 kids daily. Her thriving nonprofit, Amazima Ministries International, connects each child to a sponsor whose $25-a-month contribution provides tuition, school supplies, three meals a day, medical care, and spiritual discipleship.[214]

NOTE
Whether we realize it or not, we all want to lead our lives for a higher purpose

Not surprisingly, the choice to use the term *amazima*, which is the word for "truth" in Luganda (the native tongue of those Katie serves in Uganda), derives from Katie's unceasing desire to put her faith in action.[215] Although some critics question the sustainability of her efforts in this distant African nation, she remains convinced she's exactly where she should be. Her countless memories of visiting children with distended bellies in the hospital, or of anxiously awaiting the results of an HIV test that may forever seal a young boy's fate, empower her to keep fighting for those the world has chosen to leave behind.

Today, Katie is going as strong as ever. Her four-bedroom rented house serves as a haven and shelter for children who lack a positive role model in their lives. It's a place where an adult is real, welcoming, and above all, loving. Her tireless effort in drawing attention to the terribly high number of orphans across the globe—143 million and growing—is building value into others lives each and every day.

On a continent far, far away from her once-comfortable existence, Katie Davis is proving herself in every sense of the word to be a leader intent on taking the initiative to accept responsibility for leading the positive change she wants to see. Her willingness to walk differently in the world confirming her belief that life was designed to be lived to the fullest—all we have to do, in Katie's own words, "is get up and embrace it."[216]

The Fruits of Embracing Responsibility

Have you ever noticed how often we find ourselves gravitating toward responsible people in our lives? Those who choose not to blame, pass the buck, or waste time skirting their duties or ignoring opportunities to try to make good things happen. Those who choose instead to do everything they possibly can to promote solutions to society's most pressing problems.

I know I certainly have.

But for all this talk about the importance of embracing responsibility, why does it really matter? For one, it's because without someone accepting responsibility for putting into motion the change they want to see, positive progress just can't happen. If everyone abdicates ownership, who's left to do the work to help create conditions for things to get moving in a desired direction? Think about this. If Dr. Parker had not stepped up to accept the responsibility for helping to serve the poorest of the poor in Africa, where would the tens of thousands of people Mercy Ships has served be today? How much longer would the blight of segregation been allowed to continue if Rosa Parks had not made her courageous, one-person stand against the prevailing social norms on that bus in Montgomery, Alabama, in 1955?

Or, what would have happened to the one hundred thousand–plus Jewish people Raoul Wallenberg saved from the death camps in World War II? Where would Connie Henderson be today if Kelley, the part-time repo man in Dallas, had not exercised the courage to stretch outside his comfort zone to help her get back on her feet? And how many more orphans would have no one to care for them if Katie Davis had not risked leaving her comfortable life in America to serve children in rural Africa?

As we've seen in example after example throughout this book, we all have something to offer to help heal our hurting world. And here's the best part. We don't have to take any special course; graduate from any special program; or possess a particular rank, title, or position to get to work improving things in our homes, workplaces, worship spaces, or communities. We simply need to dig deep within ourselves to muster the moral courage to risk making different, more empowering choices. Doing unto others as we ourselves would like others to do for us by *setting an example* worth emulating.

Parting Thoughts

Dr. Martin Luther King Jr. once boldly proclaimed, "Cowardice asks the question: Is it safe? Expediency asks the question: Is it politic? Vanity asks the question: Is it popular? But conscience asks the question: Is it right? And there comes a time when one must take a position that is neither safe, nor politic, nor popular—but one must take it simply because it is right."

There is much to be done in the righting of our world, and time is certainly of the essence. We can wait for someone else to act, or we can choose to kick start the process of positive change ourselves.

By adopting the same simple practices the world's most unlikely, but immensely effective change agents have been using for thousands of years to upend the status quo, we too can show an ever-watching world how anyone can choose to make a profoundly positive difference. Anyone, that is, who is willing to:

- *Think differently* about their role in the world by doing something to *lead the change* they want to see in their surroundings;

- *Act boldly* in capitalizing on *opportunities* to build value into others lives; and,
- *Be the best version of themselves* by choosing to be *a force for good* right where they are today?

In the end, the legend of the willing burden bearer, which derives from the reknown Sermon on the Mount, serves as a blueprint for how we should strive to lead our lives. In the words of psychologist J. T. Fuller, "If you were to take the sum total of all authoritative articles ever written by the most qualified of psychologists and psychiatrists on the subject of mental hygiene—if you were to combine them and refine them and cleave out the excess verbiage—if you were to take the whole of the meat and none of the parsley, and if you were to have unadulterated bits of pure scientific knowledge concisely expressed by the most capable of living poets, you would have an awkward and incomplete summation of the Sermon on the Mount. And it would suffer immeasurably through comparison."[217]

For nearly two thousand years, the world has been holding in its hands the key to creating conditions for humanity to consistently flourish and thrive, individually and communally. The oft-used but little understood phrase, willingly "go the second mile" revealing that the solution to our society's challenges, big or small, is already present, invisible in plain sight. It is found in the examples of those everyday citizens who are unafraid to reject mediocrity and embrace excellence as their preferred way of walking in the world.

No special training required.

No more mediocre me.

Dream Big Dreams

*Freedom has its life in the hearts, the actions, the spirit of
men and so it must be daily earned and refreshed—else like a
flower cut from its life-giving roots, it will wither and die.*
—Dwight D. Eisenhower

The late president Ronald Reagan, at his inaugural address
in 1981, insightfully shared how "from time to time we've
been tempted to believe that society has become too complex
to be managed by self-rule, that government by an elite group is
superior to government for, by, and of the people. But if no one
among us is capable of government himself, then who among us has
the capacity to govern someone else?"[218] The former Commander-
in-Chief continued, adding how "all of us together—in and out of
government—must bear the burden. The solution we seek must be
equitable...our concerns must be for a special-interest group that has
long been neglected. It knows no societal boundaries, or ethnic or
racial divisions, and it crosses political party lines. It is made up of men
and women who raise our food, tend our children, keep our homes,

and heal us when we're sick. Professionals, industrialists, shopkeepers, clerks, cabbies, and truck drivers. They are, in short, 'we the people.' This breed called Americans."[219]

What Reagan was speaking to was the need for every American to respond to the warnings occurring in their spheres of influence by rejecting apathy and embracing action. He was reminding each of us who call ourselves citizens of this great country that the status quo had to go and the fastest, most effective way to make that happen was to roll up our sleeves and accept personal responsibility to get to work ourselves. Most importantly, he was reminding each and every one of us how co-creating the kind of country we desire and deserve is first and foremost an inside job. Something made possible because of our ability to dream big dreams and get busy pursuing those dreams.

The American Dream

Deep down in the hearts of those who call themselves "American" exists a shared ideal that we commonly refer to as "the American Dream." It is a dream that has shone brightly at times and has faded in others. It is a dream that reflects how things could be different if we choose to operate at our individual and collective *best*.

Have you ever stopped to define this dream for yourself? Have you ever paused and asked, what is the American Dream to me?

One of the many wonderful things about this notion of the American Dream is that it cannot be narrowly defined. There is no one-size-fits-all interpretation. The variations in definitions abound, limited only by the number of people who choose to actively attempt to define it.

Yet although the concept of the American Dream can't be tightly bound or distilled into a simple list of detailed descriptors, I do believe several characteristics cannot be denied. These include:

- **Dreaming.** We are at our best when we are free to use our imagination, the birthplace of our dreams, to develop creative solutions to daunting challenges.
- **Acting.** We are at our best when we actively do something to make our dreams a reality, willfully exercising the personal

responsibility to lead the change we want to see occur in our surroundings.

- **A Higher Purpose.** We are at our best when we choose to lead our lives not for ourselves but for a higher purpose.

Dreaming. When the earliest settlers of this land set off from the Old World seeking refuge in the new, they did so to escape fear and coercion, tyranny and oppression, famine and fighting. Our forefathers wanted things to be different. So they mustered *the strength of character* to set out to establish a new life in a new land in the belief that this place, America, would be the place where they could grow into the best version of themselves. Their measure of success was less a by-product of focusing on how to overcome their limitations and more a function of tapping into their imagination to develop creative solutions to even the most perplexing problems. Proof positive that we are a country of dreamers who are at our best not when we blindly conform to the norm, but rather when we are thinking more broadly and creatively about our circumstances.

Acting. The *freedom* to dream of a better life is insufficient in itself to propel us forward. We must *do something* to transform these dreams into practical action. Those leaders before us who have shed precious blood at Bunker Hill, Valley Forge, Bull Run, Châteaux-Thierry in the Argonne, Iwo Jima, Guadalcanal, Korea, Vietnam, Iraq, and Afghanistan did so for a reason. That is, they recognized that speaking about an ideal and standing up to preserve a cherished way of life are two very distinct things. Rhetoric alone will not make our dreams a reality. Action is required to ultimately move things solidly forward. But as always, someone must lead the change and accept responsibility to go first, to show others the way.

A Higher Purpose. It is easy to make an idol of routine, finding security within the boundaries we build around our lives. Although each day contains twenty-four hours, every single one of these presents an opportunity to contribute to a purpose larger than ourselves. For me personally, that higher purpose is to do what I can, when I can, where I can to try to build value into others' lives each and every day in a multitude of ways. My greatest satisfaction derives from using my God-given talents and skills to be a force for good in my home, workplace, worship space, and community.

The more important point to make, however, is that I know I can't accomplish this alone. My contribution in itself is small, particularly when you consider the magnitude of challenges facing our nation and our planet today. But I, like the founding leaders of our nation before me, recognize there is a higher power, *God*, eager and willing to help make our dreams a reality.

All we have to do is ask.

Since America's first days, God has been central to the ideal we term the American Dream. Without God, there is no America, and without America, there can be no American Dream. This fact is affirmed both in the Declaration of Independence and the Bill of Rights. Our reliance on God first, as a nation and as a people, is deemed the foundation of all other freedoms. Take that away and eventually all freedom, all liberty, is lost.

So what does it mean to rely on God as our true source of strength?

It certainly doesn't guarantee us the American Dream we so often visualize in our minds. You know, the one in which we live in a large home, drive an expensive or exotic car (or cars), or have our name on the marquee or our face on TV. Nor does it imply things will always be easy or work out as we wish. Ours is, after all, a fallen world in which illness, disease, divorce, poverty, heartache, and death are very, very real occurrences.

What it does help us better understand is that those wise men and women who established America centuries ago knew they could not even hope of achieving their dream of creating a country that valued life, liberty, and the pursuit of happiness for all its citizens alone. They needed God to guide them in pulling off something so bold, so risky, and, dare I say, so *different*. So they chose to place their trust in God for achieving their American Dream. And today, centuries later, our nation stands as a powerful and persuasive example to an ever-watching world of how being different can be good. In fact, very, very good.

Parting Thoughts

Nolan Bushnell, the creator of the Atari video game system, once stated, "Everyone who's ever taken a shower has an idea. It's the person who gets out of the shower, dries off, and does something about it who makes a difference."[220]

Ultimately, the American Dream is a treasure buried deep within each and every one of us. But like anything of immense value, this treasure is of little good if it stays buried. It can only be enjoyed if it is discovered, uncovered, and ultimately shared. Leaving each of us to wonder what could be accomplished if more *leaders* today choose to take God up on his standing offer to use each of us as catalysts for positive change, right where we are?

No special training required.

I'm convinced God has been patiently waiting since the day he created this great country for us to realize the solution we are looking for to resolve every obstacle to achieving the American Dream is already present, *invisible in plain sight.*

It's simply a matter of looking in the mirror and discovering it within yourself.

MediocreMe.Com

I wrote Mediocre Me to convince you to think more broadly about *your* important role in the world. My ultimate goal is to help people everywhere recognize that no matter where we find ourselves in the social hierarchy, be it as a parent, pastor, patrolman, soldier, salesman, senator, or anywhere else for that matter, we already possess everything required to make a profoundly positive difference in our surroundings. However, we must *choose* to exercise the personal responsibility to *lead the change* we want to see in our spheres of influence.

With this said, I want to hear how you (and others like you) are using your personal power and authority to make going the second mile second nature, right where you are. At the Mediocre Me website (www. MediocreMe.com), you can share your story and learn about how other positive change catalysts like you are making our country and our planet a better, brighter place to live, work, play, and pray, one choice at a time.

It is my sincere hope that maybe, in the process of sharing, your positive example will motivate someone else to choose to take their own first, courageous step in a different but empowering new direction. Compelling them to discover for themselves how leading one's life in a more excellent way begins by opening ourselves to thinking differently, acting boldly, and committing to becoming the best version of ourselves possible—one opportunity at a time.

Notes, Cautions & Warnings Summary

Notes

- One of the primary roles of a leader is to help guide others toward a future they can influence, liberating them from a past they cannot change
- The true leaders in our society are those whose performance and attitude exceed our expectations when the chips are down and hard things need to get done
- Leadership…is meant to be a responsibility we choose to fulfill—one opportunity at a time
- We can accomplish just about anything in life if we are willing to reject mediocrity and face our fear of change head-on
- Leadership is less about position and more about disposition
- The world in which we live is largely of our own making…We are, by the choices we routinely make, the primary architects of our realities
- The most profound changes we can make in our lives are not outward but inward
- Role modeling is actually our preferred means of empowering ourselves and those around us to reject mediocrity and stretch ourselves in new directions

- Sociologists tell us that even the most introverted person in the world will influence at least 10,000 people in their lifetime
- To embrace responsibility means cultivating and protecting those things you are immediately accountable for in your surroundings
- Accepting responsibility for our choices actually calms our minds and clarifies our vision. It soothes our emotions and enables us to think and act more positively and constructively
- Risk taking is the willingness to be different where different can get things moving in a new, more empowering direction
- To risk failure is to embrace living life to its fullest
- Risk taking isn't about being reckless, forging forward without thought of where you're going or what you're doing
- Risk taking is the price we must be willing to pay to get things moving in a new, more empowering, direction
- You learn to overcome your fear of change by becoming more comfortable taking risks. The more risks you take, the less fear can have its way with you
- Making a positive difference in the world...results from a commitment to serving our neighbor by choosing to do small things with great love
- Compassion is...to suffer with affection for another
- Feeling valued by others is fundamental to our happiness and well being
- Conducting ourselves compassionately... can change everything
- Courage is an ideal that should fuel all people's desire and ability to live a life of purpose and meaning
- Truth is the glue that holds a sane and civilized society together
- If we choose inaction when action is clearly warranted, we confirm we don't possess the moral courage to fight for what's right when others need us most
- Hope is the first of our "emergency" virtues
- Balancing our optimism with a healthy dose of defensive pessimism...can actually insulate us from experiencing crushing disappointment
- A disciplined ego is what it takes to muster the moral courage to take prudent risks and assume responsibility for our actions

- Self-control is the ability to look outside oneself in a way that balances a healthy self-denial with a deep seated commitment to live up to a particular standard
- Although leadership can often be challenging to define, you certainly know it when you see it
- We are at our best not when we are simply serving ourselves or satisfying our agendas, but rather when we are giving the best of ourselves in service to something larger than ourselves
- The sooner we make character development a priority in our lives, the better equipped we will be to operate at peak
- Whether we realize it or not, we all want to lead our lives for a higher purpose.

Cautions

- Quite unintentionally, we fell prey to the lie that success was a right we deserved rather than a privilege we must continue to earn
- When something becomes commonplace, we have a tendency to neglect it or just plain look past it
- Experiencing some momentary brain discomfort…is a sure-tell sign you're moving in the right direction
- Regret is both an emotion as well as a punishment we administer to ourselves;
- Our words possess immense power
- The discomfort wrought by our stretching outside our comfort zones is so significant that we are actually two-and-a-half times more prone to stay put than to act
- Leadership is not a safe haven
- Truth is not something we can hide from
- Although building on strength is preferred, ignoring those things in our lives that are not working as they should will not make them go away
- Gratitude is rarely our first response
- For all the benefits of gratefulness, it's just not a virtue we naturally put into practice

Warnings

- The status quo strives to keep us squarely in our comfort zones and persuades us to accept mediocrity as the norm
- Mediocrity is insidious and dangerous…it clouds our thinking and hinders our actions, cultivating doubt of the future
- Passivity…does nothing but undermine our potential, destroy our families, damage our businesses, ruin our communities, and spoil our legacies
- Fear…serves as the proverbial canary in the coal mine that alerts us to potential danger
- It's the inaction regrets we remember most
- Without compassion we are bound to feel alone, especially during those times we need others help the most
- Moral courage is only exemplified by those who possess the internal strength of character to do what's right, no matter the potential cost to self
- One of our greatest hindrances to becoming a courageous leader… is our natural aversion to experiencing loss
- When the pressure to conform to what others are expecting or demanding of us begins to supplant our own sense of what's right and wrong…watch out
- Cognitive scientists have found that when it comes to our initial reaction toward change, our brains are actually wired to work against us
- Despite being a biological mechanism to help make life easier for us, the status-quo bias actually trips us up
- The tendency to be more optimistic than realistic is a common trap people tend to fall into
- Hopelessness clouds the way we look at things, making us suspicious of the future and negative about the present
- An unchecked ego can quickly get the better of us, distorting our perspective of who we are, what we are capable of, and of the role others play in both our success and failure.

Notes

Acknowledgments

The list of people who made this book possible is long. Each deserves a standing ovation for their patience and persistence.

To my wife, Holly—you are the love of my life. Everything I've achieved is a direct reflection of your grace and unwavering support and commitment. Know that I thank God every day for allowing me to share this time on earth with you.

To my sons, Taylor and Brandon—nothing gives me as much joy as being your Dad. You are both amazing young men with an abundance of talent to share with the world. I could not be prouder of you both.

To my mom and dad, Jean and Patricia Michel—thank you for your example, your prayers, and your encouragement in every area of my life. It's made all the difference.

To my brother and sister, Frank and Catherine Michel—better siblings there are none.

To Jean—from the deserts of Iraq to the cornfields of Illinois, your keen insight and trustworthy counsel made all the difference in seeing this project to completion. I'm blessed to call you friend.

To my editors, Amanda and Georganne—you are skilled word surgeons who helped transform a dream into reality. Your attention to detail is exceeded only by your wisdom. I'm grateful.

Father John Kinney, aka Padre, your steady stream of prayer is like a sturdy wall. Thanks for being such a great partner in delivering our message to anyone who will listen.

To the rest of the manuscript review team, Sonya, Jackie, Amy, Matt, Doug and Mark, if a better team of trusted friends exists, I've never seen it.

To my publishing family at Morgan James—thanks for believing in me and giving me this shot. Your personal and professional support for this book has gone above and beyond the call of duty.

To all those authors, teachers, leaders, and change artists whose attitudes and actions have influenced my thinking—where my words sound like yours, forgive me. You deserve the credit for helping me make Medicore Me come to life.

And last, but certainly not least, to all those Soldiers, Sailors, Airmen, Marines, and Coast Guardsmen who inspire me every day by your acts of selfless service—you remind me why wearing the uniform of our nation is such a privilege, indeed.

About the Author

John E. Michel is a widely recognized expert in culture, strategy & individual and organizational change. An accomplished unconventional leader and proven status quo buster, he has successfully led several multi-billion dollar transformation efforts and his award-winning work has been featured in a wide variety of articles and journals, including the Harvard Business Review. In addition to serving our nation as an active-duty Brigadier General in the United States Air Force, John enjoys helping people learn to walk differently in the world so they can become the best version of themselves possible. He is blessed to be married to the most patient person on the planet and together, they have two amazing sons. You are encouraged to learn more about John at his website, www.MedicoreMe.com

Endnotes

1. As a sampling of the many challenges facing our society, consider these startling statistics, gathered from a host of Government-sponsored websites during the time I wrote this book: Unemployment in America hovers close to 10 percent. Debt is soaring and despair and hopelessness are skyrocketing. Our nation experiences sixty suicides an hour and over fifteen thousand teens use drugs every day. Every twenty-four hours, 3,506 teens run away. Rape is up 14 percent, crime 65 percent, and the rate of broken homes and shattered lives continues to increase, with divorce accounting for 46 percent of all marriages.

2. Lydia Saad, "Democrats and Republicans Agree That US Morals Are Subpar," *Gallup News Service*, May 21, 2004, http://www.gallup.com/poll/11758/democrats-republicans-agree-us-morals-subpar.aspx.

3. Harvard Kennedy School, "Poll Shows Americans Still Disappointed in Leaders," news release, October 28, 2010, http://www.hks.harvard.edu/news-events/news/press-releases/pr-cpl-nli-oct10.

4. *Newsweek*, September 19, 2011, 45.

5. Ronald Heifetz, Alexander Grashow, and Marty Linsky, *The Practice of Adaptive Leadership* (Boston: Harvard Business Press, 2009), 28.

6. It may be interesting to note that there is no word for service in Greek or in Latin. The closest word, however, is *charizo*, meaning "to choose to do something good." The Latin word that best fits service is *beneficium*, meaning "an act tending to the benefit of another," or to put it simply, "doing good deeds."

7. The concept of knowing the way, showing the way and going the way was first introduced by leadership expert John C. Maxwell.

8. Dennis Rainey, *Stepping up: A Call to Courageous Manhood* (Little Rock, AR: Family Life Publishing, 2011), 113.

9. What I find particularly interesting is that, almost twenty years before the Declaration of Independence was penned, one of our nation's greatest leaders, John Adams, at the ripe old age of twenty-eight, shared these insightful words: "In the state of nature, every man has a right to think and act according to the dictates of his own mind, which in that state, are subject to no other control and can be commanded by no other power than the laws and ordinances of the great Creator of all things...He therefore is the truest friend to the Liberty of his country who tries most to promote its virtue...The sum of all is, if we would most truly enjoy this gift of Heaven, let us become a virtuous people." See Verna M. Halls, *The Christian History of the Constitution* (San Francisco: Foundation for American Christian Education, 1980), 365–366.

10. I am indebted to personal and organizational change expert Dr. Price Pritchett, whose many books on change have helped shape my thinking about the many dynamic ways we as leaders can help individuals smartly address change in their own lives. For purposes of this chapter, I was particularly influenced by his guide entitled *Mind Shift: The Employee Handbook for Understanding the Changing World of Work* (Dallas: Pritchett & Associates, 1996). Additionally, I recommend you visit his website at www.pritchett.com to explore the host of outstanding material he and his firm offer in helping position you and your organization to wisely navigate change.

11. This story was adapted from Sherri W. Fisher, *Against All Odds: Broadening and Building Resilience Across the Life Span*, available at: http://pospsyched.wordpress.com/2009/05/18/against-all-odds-broadening-and-building-resilience-across-the-life-span.

12. "Status quo," Answers Corporation, http://www.answers.com/topic/status-quo.

13. Clifton, D. O., & Harter, J. K. (2003), Investing in Strengths. In A. K.S. Cameron, B.J.E. Dutton, & C.R.E Quinn (Eds), *Positive Organizational Scholarship: Foundations of a New Discipline* (pp. 111-121). San Francisco: Berrett-Koehler Publishers Inc.

14. *The Armed Forces Officer* (US Department of Defense, 1950), 1.

15. *Counterintuitive,* according to the dictionary, means "contrary to what common sense would suggest." *AudioEnglish.net*, s.v. "counterintuitive," http://www.audioenglish.net/dictionary/counterintuitive.htm.

16. *Anastasis* is Greek for "resurrection."

17. The Parkers' two children, Carys and Wesley, also call the ship home, along with fifty other children of thirty-five nationalities.

18. Excerpted from Dr. Parker's blog video speech at http://www. mercyships.org/video/entry/connections-march-2011, accessed March 15, 2011.

19. Excerpted from Dr. Parker's blog video speech at http://www. mercyships.org/video/entry/connections-march-2011, accessed March 15, 2011.

20. Many Africans with deformities or diseases live alone, hiding their faces behind scarves. They all stand in long lines in the hot sun for a chance to be evaluated by the *Anastasis* medical team and, hopefully, deemed eligible for surgery.

21. The inspiration for this story came from Max Lucado's sermon, *Enough of this Fear*. The sermon can be accessed at oakhillschurch.com mobile media page.

22. Max Lucado shared these insightful words in his sermon, *Enough of this Fear*.

23. Jack B. Haskins and Alice Kendrick, *Successful Advertising Research Methods* (Lincolnwood, IL: NTC Business Books, 1993).

24. Joseph LeDoux, a professor at the Center for Neural Science at New York University, writes in his book, *The Emotional Brain: The Mysterious Underpinnings of Emotional Life*; how systems in the brain work in response to emotions, particularly fear. Among his fascinating findings is the work of amygdala structure within the brain. The amygdala mediates fear and other responses and actually processes information more quickly than other parts of the brain, allowing a rapid response that can save our lives before other parts of the brain have had a chance to react.

25. John C. Maxwell, *The Journey from Success to Significance* (Nashville, TN: Thomas Nelson, 2004).

26. Richard Pascale, Jerry Sternin, and Monique Sternin, *The Power of Positive Deviance: How Unlikely Innovators Solve the World's Toughest Problems* (Boston: Harvard Business Press, 2010).

27. Credit for the discovery of the deeper meaning behind this famous parable goes to Walter Wink, who does a wonderful job of describing the conditions of the era and circumstances that lead to such an interpretation in his book, *Jesus and Nonviolence: A Third Way* (Minneapolis, MN: Fortress Press, 2003).

28. The full exhortation reads, "If someone forces you to go one mile, go with him two," Matthew 5:41 (NIV). Sid Buzzell, Kenneth Boa, and Bill Perkins, eds., *The Leadership Bible: Leadership Principles from God's Word* (Grand Rapids, MI: Zondervan, 1998).

29. This practice originated from the Roman *mille passus*, or "thousand paces," which measured five thousand Roman feet (4,840 English feet or 1.475 km).

30. Remember, thousands of years ago, kings and rulers maintained their authority over conquered lands through a show of force. As a result, armies had a lot of territory to cover and, as is often the case in warfare, time is of the essence. Thus soldiers needed to move quickly. Given these challenging realities, some of the more privileged, well-to-do men brought their own slaves to help carry their packs and their weapons. The majority, however, did not possess the means. Therefore, they depended on impressed civilians to ease their burdens.

31. Wink, *Jesus and Nonviolence.*

32. The idea that our actions alter our preferences and influence our choices is known as the Free Choice Paradox and has been replicated hundreds of times in independent studies and is supported in large sets of data.

33. Rollo May, *The Courage to Create* (New York: Norton, 1994).

34. Max DePree, *Leading Without Power: Finding Hope in Serving Community* (San Francisco: Jossey-Bass, 1997). Emphasis added.

35. *Wikiversity*, s.v. "Comparison between Roman and Han Empires," last modified February 14, 2012, http://en.wikiversity.org/wiki/Comparison_between_Roman_and_Han_Empires.

36. "Lesotho Diamond Makes History," SouthAfrica.Info, http://www.southafrica.info/pls/procs/iac.page?p_t1=694&p_t2=1833&p_t3=0&p_t4=0&p_dynamic=YP&p_content_id=242524&p_site_id=38Document2, accessed October 11, 2006.

37. Victor Davis Hanson, *The Soul of Battle: From Ancient Times to the Present Day, How Three Great Liberators Vanquished Tyranny* (New York: Simon and Schuster, 1999).

38. The Boeotians, on the other hand, followed a radical practice: Wealthy horseman voluntarily shared power with average farmers and the poor, and the formal leaders of the society chose to emphasize service to others instead of focusing on ways they could benefit themselves. Their willingness to deviate from the accepted norm of society, which at the time clearly favored those with formal authority, position, and title, had a profoundly positive effect on the people, increasing national unity and ultimately making it easier to get volunteers for the army when the call to war was sounded.

39. Hanson, *The Soul of Battle.*

40. *Online Etymology Dictionary*, s.v. "revolution," by Douglas Harper, http://www.etymonline.com/index.php?term=revolution.

41. The Greek word for transformation is *metamorphoo* and literally translates as *"to change into another form."* Emphasis added.

42. Unlike revolutions, transformations rarely have a clearly defined beginning or end. There is just a noticeable development that takes place over time. It's like not seeing someone for awhile and you noticed that they lost some weight, but when you see them every day it's not so obvious.

43. Source

44. Ibid, pp. 1

45. Proverbs 4:26, TEV

46. *Phronēsis* is an Ancient Greek word for wisdom or intelligence which is a common topic of discussion in philosophy. In Aristotelian Ethics, for example in the *Nicomachean Ethics* it is distinguished from other words for wisdom as the virtue of practical thought, and is usually translated "practical wisdom", sometimes as "prudence."

47. A division is a military organization that ranges between 10,000 and 15,000 soldiers and associated equipment, and it is usually commanded by a two-star general.

48. Julie J. McGowan, "Swimming with the Sharks: Perspectives on Professional Risk Taking," *Journal of the Medical Association* 95, no. 1 (January 2007): 104–113.

49. Muhammad Najeed and Hasan Zaidi, "Benazir Bhutto: Daughter of Tragedy," *India Today*, January 7, 2008. Bhutto was assassinated on December 27, 2007, two weeks before the scheduled Pakistani general election of 2008, in which she was a leading opposition candidate for the country's presidency. In 2008 she was posthumously named one of seven winners of the United Nations Prize in the Field of Human Rights.

50. The National Transportation Safety Board determined that the cause of the accident was pilot error. The pilots failed to switch on the engines' internal ice protection systems, used reverse thrust in a snow storm prior to takeoff, and failed to abort the takeoff even after detecting a power problem while taxiing and visually identifying ice and snow buildup on the wings.

51. Neal Roese, *If Only: How to Turn Regret into an Opportunity* (New York: Broadway Books, 2005), 48.

52. Peter Sims, *Little Bets: How Breakthrough Ideas Emerge From Small Discoveries* (New York: Free Press, 2011).

53. Gail Sheehy, *Pathfinders* (New York: Bantam, 1982).

54.   Albert Bandura, "Social Learning through Imitation," (Lincoln, NE: University of Nebraska Press, 1962).

55.   Sociologists and psychologists tell us Modeling Theory operates in three simple steps: (1) You observe a model; (2) You imitate the model's actions, and (3) You get a consequence.

56.   Derek Ashford, Simon Bennett, and Keith Davids, "Observational Modeling Effects for Movement Dynamics and Movement Outcome Measures across Differing Task Constraints: A Meta-Analysis," *Journal of Motor Behavior* 38, 185–205.

57.   Albert Bandura, *Social Learning Theory* (Englewood Cliffs, NJ: Prentice Hall, 1977).

58.   There are three core concepts at the heart of social learning theory. First is the idea that people can learn through observation. Next is the idea that internal mental states are an essential part of this process. Finally, this theory recognizes that just because something has been learned, it does not mean that it will result in a change in behavior.

59.   www.newhopewauchula.org/.../wnl-eph518-20-undertheinfluence.pdf

60.   Pritchett, Deep Strengths.

61.   Scott Farnell, "How Hall of Fame Cowboy Roger Staubach's Charity Is Different," *The Dallas Morning News*, www.dallasnews.com/sports/dollars-cowboys/headlines/20110118-how-hall-of-fame-cowboy-roger-staubachs-charity-is-different.ece, accessed December 12, 2011.

62.   The state that arises when we experience inconsistency in our surroundings is called *dissonance.* Dissonance is simply a technical term for the cognitive, emotional, physiological, and behavioral state that arises when things do not go as we expected them to.

63.   Elmer Bendiner, *The Fall of Fortresses: A Personal Account of the Most Daring, and Deadly, American Air Battles of World War II* (New York: Putnam, 1980).

64.   Alexandre Havard, *Virtuous Leadership: An Agenda for Personal Excellence* (New York: Scepter, 2007).

65.   Joseph S. Nye Jr., *The Powers to Lead* (New York: Oxford University Press, 2008).

66.   Nye, "The Powers to Lead."

67.   Stephen Kendrick, Alex Kendrick, and Randy Alcorn, *The Resolution For Men* (Nashville, TN: B&H Publishing Group, 2011).

68.   This story was adapted from an article by Steve Blow, "What Possessed Repo Man? 'A God Thing,'" *Dallas Morning News*, December 24, 2010, pages 1B and 2B.

69. Ibid.

70. "Albert Einstein Quotes: Insanity," BrainyQuote, http://www.brainyquote.com/quotes/quotes/a/alberteins133991.html.

71. Astin, A. W., & Astin, H. S. (2000). *Leadership reconsidered: Engaging higher education in social change*. Battle Creek, MI: W. K. Kellogg Foundation

72. Confucius lived between 551-479 B.C. His teachings are considered the most influential in the history of Chinese thought and civilization. His moral and political philosophy, with its keen focus on leadership and education, became the official religion of China by the second century B.C and essential study in the two thousand plus years since.

73. John Templeton, *Agape Love: A Tradition Found in Eight World Religions* (Radnor, PA: Templeton Foundation Press, 1999).

74. It is also within this school of Confucian thought that we see a precursor to the modern western idea of service.

75. Over time, the concept of *jen* underwent a transformation. Meng Tzu, a student of Confucius, expanded its meaning to emphasize further how leaders had certain obligations toward their people and if those obligations were not properly fulfilled, then those being led were absolved of any loyalty to the leader. In other words, *Jen* is a radical concept that served to remind everyone that a leader could be stripped of the privilege of leading if they lost focus on what matters most— serving others.

76. John Templeton, *Agape Love: A Tradition Found in Eight World Religions* (Radnor, PA: Templeton Foundation Press, 1999).

77. Love is a word with more meanings than most of us realize. From the Greeks we get the word, *philia*, and *philadelphos*, meaning brotherly love; *filial* love is the love of child for parent and vice versa; divine love is the love of God for all, commonly expressed as *Agape*; and from the Greek word *eros* we get erotic love.

78. R. Hooker, "Chinese Philosophy," World Civilizations Online (1996), accessed March 31 2008; available from http://www.wsu.edu/~dee/CHPHIL/MOTZU.HTM. Mo Tzu (470 to 391 B.C.) expanded on Confucius' ideas of *jen*, emphasizing the ethical principle of universal love, or loving every human being equally. To Mo Tzu, fellow human beings should provide for the weak and the hungry, avoid hurtful activities such as war or profiteering, and avoid any activity that did not take care of someone or something. Righteousness, or *jen,* for Mo Tzu, was not achieved by extending help only to one's family but by helping others in need.

79. It's interesting to note that the word *submit* comes from the Greek *hupotasso*, meaning to subordinate to, obey, or become subject to another person. When done voluntarily in love, submission to others is an act of humility and service that seeks to bring out the best in those around us.

80. http://www.science-spirit.org/article_detail.php?article_id=192

81. Christopher Peterson & Martin E. P. Seligman, *Character Strengths and Virtues: A Handbook and Classification* (New York: Oxford University Press, 2004).

82. http://www.nytimes.com/2009/02/05/us/politics/05text-prayer.html?_r=1&pagewanted=print

83. This quote comes from the Christian Old Testament (Leviticus 19:18) and is also found in the New Testament Gospels.

84. This quote comes from the Jewish Torah,

85. This phrase comes from the Islamic Hadith,

86. The Golden Rule or the ethic of reciprocity is found in the scriptures of nearly every religion. It is often regarded as the most concise and general principle of ethics.

87. Love 146 was founded in 2002 by a small group of friends committed to loving the most broken people, sexually exploited children. Traveling to Southeast Asia to see the sex trade industry firsthand, they posed as customers in a particular brothel. The small group quickly discovered the intense, sordid reality of child sex slavery. Along with actual customers, they were marshaled into a room filled with little girls in red dresses each identified not by name, but by number. The girls were gathered around small TVs, blankly entertaining themselves in between "work." All but one, that is: Number 146. Unlike the others, this little girl stared back at the customers—with an intensity that communicated she still had fight left in her. A short time later, the group returned to the brother, this time accompanied by local authorities. They rescued scores of children that night, but number 146 was nowhere to be found. Nor was she ever seen again. In honor of the brave little girl in the red dresses memory, the organization selected 146 as their name. Please go to www.love146.org to check out this incredible group of people.

88. Academic research demonstrates that giving to others benefits people physically and emotionally. An article in the May 1988 issue of American Health magazine described a study in Michigan that showed regular volunteer work increases life expectancy. The study found that men who did no volunteer work were two-and-a-half times more likely to die during the study than men who volunteered at least once a week.

89. Retrieved at http://www.sermonillustrations.com/a-z/l/love.htm

90. Dutton, J. E. & Ragins, B. R. (2007). *Exploring Positive Relationships at work*. Mahwah, NJ: Erlbaum.

91. Pratt, M. G., & Dirks, K. T. (2007). Rebuilding Trust and Restoring Positive Relationships: A Commitment-based view of trust. In J. E. Dutton & B. R. Ragins (Eds), *Exploring Positive Relationships at work* (pp. 117-16). Mahwah, NJ: Erlbaum.

92. As a citizenry, Americans are at once charitable and stingy. According to the National Philanthropic Trust, 89 percent of American households give to charity. Sounds impressive, but think about this: on average, we donate just 1.9 percent of our household income.

93. Martin Luther King Jr., shared a similar sentiment when he said, "I have decided to stick with love. Hate is too great a burden to bear."

94. Colonel Juan Ayala, Advisor Duty is Mentally Taxing and Intensely Personal. *Marine Corps Gazette*. March 2008. pg. 53.

95. Larry Gallagher, The Compassion Instinct. *Ode Magazine*, July/August 2011. Pp. 22.

96. The English definition of "compassion" denotes affinity for and sorrow for the sufferings of another and is defined as "a feeling of sorrow for the pain or misfortunes of another that inclines one to help."

97. Admittedly, the reasons for why young people turn to the streets for survival are well-documented and the group I spent time with was certainly no different. As data bears consistently bears out, many young people who turn to the streets do so as a result of broken homes in which they are no longer wanted, are victims of sexual exploitation, drug and alcohol abuse, and a host of others unfortunate realities.

98. Scottish philosopher, historian, economist and essayist David Hume, in his classic work, *A Treatise on Human Nature*, spoke of this same misguided quest as the "is-ought" fallacy. Observing how many people infer the way something "ought" to be from the way it actually "is" when in fact, this is exactly inverse of the way we should think.

99. Jim Wallis. *Rediscovering Values: On Wall Street, Main Street and Your Street*. Howard Books. New York: NY. 2010. p. 113.

100. Neil D. Weinstein, Unrealistic Optimism about Susceptibility to Health Problems: Conclusions from a Community-Wide Sample, *Journal of Behavioral Medicine, 10*, no. 5 (1987). 481-500.

101. This innate desire to see the world as it should be, know in psychology circles as possessing an attitude of positive expectancy, is actually a huge asset. Both calling out our potential and alerting us to opportunities to use our influence for good.

102. Jane e. Dutton, Peter J. Frost, Monica C. Worline, Jacob M. Lilius, and Jason M. Kanov, Leading in Times of Trauma, *Harvard Business Review*, January 2002. P. 56.

103. Kurt S. Cameron. Organizational virtuousness and performance. In K. S. Cameron , J. E. Dutton, & R. E. Quinn (Eds), *Positive Organizational Scholarship* (pp. 48-65). 2003. San Francisco: Berrett-Koehler.

104. Adapted from a story found at http://www.uucpa.org/sermons_02-03/sermon030302.html

105. Lucado, *Applause of Heaven*.

106. Lee H. Yearley, *Mencius and Aquinas: Theories of Virtue and Conceptions of Courage* (Albany: State University of New York Press, 1990).

107. Long before the development of the Aristotelian thought, which still informs much of the Western world's views on these topics, ancient Chinese philosophers were exploring them in earnest. In fact, Mencius, writing almost twenty-five hundred years ago, was the first to expand the long-held view of courage and the role it plays in effective leadership—both of self and others.

108. Gordon Trowbridge, "Marine Sacrifices His Life for Others in Grenade Blast," *Seattle Times*, November 20, 2004, http://seattletimes.nwsource.com/html/nationworld/2002096428_hero20.html.; Oliver North, "Hero in Fallujah: Marine Laid Himself on Top of Grenade to Save Rest of Squad," *Human Events,* December 16, 2004, http://www.humanevents.com/article.php?id=6062.

109. "Navy to Name Ships after Servicemen with Local Ties," *KGTV San Diego*, February 15, 2012, http://www.10news.com/news/30467383/detail.html.

110. Rushworth M. Kidder and Martha Bracy, "Moral Courage," (white paper, Institute for Global Ethics, 2001), 5, http://ww2.faulkner.edu/admin/websites/jfarrell/moral_courage_11-03-2001.pdf.

111. Richard Rashke, *Stormy Genius: The Life of Aviation Maverick Bill Lear* (New York: Houghton Mifflin, 1985).

112. Inspired by a single-seat Swiss strike fighter aircraft, the FFA P-16 was flown as a prototype in April 1955 but was never put into production. Lear recruited a group of Swiss aircraft designers and engineers to transform the fighter's wing and basic airframe design into the cornerstone of a revolutionary aircraft—originally named the SAAC-23, but soon renamed the Learjet 23 Continental.

113. The entire Learjet program from inception to certification cost Lear $12 million. The Learjet yielded $52 million in sales its first year.

114. Rashke, *Stormy Genius.*

115. Ori Brafman and Rom Brafman, *Sway: The Irresistible Pull of Irrational Behavior* (New York: Doubleday, 2008), 19.

116. In economics and decision theory, loss aversion refers to people's tendency to strongly prefer avoiding losses to acquiring gains. There are few feelings that can actually be measured by psychologists, but the feelings we have around loss and gain are two that can be measured.

117. Richard Rapaport, "Jonestown and City Hall Slayings Eerily Linked in Time and Memory," *San Francisco Chronicle*, November 16, 2003.

118. Erwin Lutzer, *When a Nation Forgets God* (Chicago: Moody Press, 2010), 22.

119. Bill Robinson, *Incarnate Leadership: 5 Leadership Lessons from the Life of Jesus* (Grand Rapids, MI: Zondervan Publishers, 2009).

120. Davis S. Alberts and Richard E. Hayes, *Power to the Edge: Command and Control in the Information Age* (Arlington, VA: CCRP Publications, 2003).

121. The practice of sailing past one another is formally known as maneuvering broadside and refers to how the ships would align themselves in parallel in order to face off against one another in battle.

122. Alberts and Hayes, *Power to the Edge.*

123. David L. Evans, *MG (Ret) Benjamin J. Butler: A Historical Perspective of Leadership on the Battlefield* (Carlisle, PA: US Army War College, 1998).

124. There are two great forms of human change: learning and persuasion. Psychologists typically define learning as any change in behavior not caused by accident, development, or injury. The emphasis here is on pure behavior change. Persuasion, on the other hand, is a means of interacting with others that induces them to change. It's about using our personal influence to compel others to voluntarily change how they think and how they act.

125. Michael O'Hare, Lawrence Bacow, and Debra Sanderson, *Facility Siting and Public Opposition* (New York: Van Nostrand Reinhold, 1983).

126. Tom Costello, "The Seeds of Change: Serendipity and Social Movements" (lecture, National Library of Australia, Canberra, Australia, October 6, 2005).

127. John S. Hammond, Ralph L. Keeney, and Howard Raiffa, "The Hidden Traps in Decision Making," *Harvard Business Review*, September/ October 1998, 3.

128. Cognitive bias is a phenomenon studied in cognitive science and social psychology that helps explain why people make the choices they make, or don't make. The notion of cognitive biases was first introduced by

Amos Tversky and Daniel Kahneman in 1972 out of their experiences studying people who were unable to reason intuitively with the greater orders of magnitude. They and their colleagues demonstrated a host of replicable ways in which human judgments and decisions differ from rational choice theory—what they termed *heuristics*. These studies in heuristics and cognitive bias served as the foundation for further work in the area of behavioral economics, ultimately earning Kahneman a Nobel Prize in 2002. For further study on this topic, I strongly suggest you explore the following article: D. Kahneman and A. Tversky, "Subjective Probability: A Judgment of Representativeness," *Cognitive Psychology* 3 (1972), 430–454.

129. Researchers have concluded that when faced with new options, people prefer to stick with the status-quo alternative. This bias, however, is not a mistake that, once pointed out, is easily recognized and remedied. This hardwired bias is considerably more subtle and tough to shake. Please see William Samuelson and Richard Zeckhauser, "Status Quo Bias in Decision Making," *Journal of Risk and Uncertainty* 1 (1988): 7–59, for additional information on the status quo bias.

130. http://www.sas.upenn.edu/sasalum/newsltr/winter98/shore.html, p. 2

131. SOS has employed a host of innovative and entrepreneurial strategies — including food assistance, nutrition education programs and the treatment of malnutrition, the promotion of economic independence for individuals and communities, and advocacy. Please visit *http://www. strength.org to learn more about this inspiring and impressive organization.*

132. Most of these people would never consider themselves political activists. As the heroes of the 1960s were those who demonstrated for civil rights, perhaps the heroes of our generation will be those who are demonstrating their own civil responsibilities.

133. Derived from *http://www.strength.org*

134. Recently, the U.S. Census Bureau released a report stating the rate of poverty in America has climbed to its highest level in more than 20 years. That's 46 million people in the U.S. living at or below the poverty line. It's also the largest total number since the bureau started tracking poverty in 1959. And there's more. A third of Americans being served at food banks are under eighteen years old; this year over 12 million children in our country are worried about going hungry. And the number is many times that amount worldwide.

135. Tony Schwartz, Save us from Our Strengths, *HBR Blog Network*, http://blogs.hbr.org/schwartz/2012/09/save-us-from-our-strengths.html?utm_medium=refernce, accessed 09/28/2012.

136. Tony Schwartz, Save us from Our Strengths, *HBR Blog Network,* http://
blogs.hbr.org/schwartz/2012/09/save-us-from-our-strengths.html?utm_
medium=refernce, accessed 09/28/2012.

137. This metaphor was inspired by Kathy L. Casper, "Thoughts on Life,
Liberty, and the Pursuit of Happiness" (1996) http://www.freelaunch.
com/essays/liberty.html.

138. This railway system included the bridge made notorious by the movie,
Bridge on the River Kwai.

139. Ernest Gordon, *Through the Valley of the River Kwai* (New York: Harper
& Row, 1962).

140. Ernest Gordon went on to become an ordained minister, highly
acclaimed author (his famous book *Through the Valley of the Kwai*
was made into the movie *To End All Wars)*, and dean of the chapel at
Princeton University. Throughout his life he focused his teachings on
how it is possible to find hope in the most impossible of places.

141. This story was inspired by a short story in Max Lucado's *The Applause of
Heaven* (Nashville, TN: Thomas Nelson, 1990).

142. Merriam-Webster's Collegiate Dictionary, s.v. "hope."

143. Joan Chittister, *Scarred by Struggle, Transformed by Hope* (Cambridge:
Eerdmans, 2005), 103.

144. James Stockdale and Sybil Stockdale, *In Love and War* (New York:
Harper & Row, 1984).

145. Ibid.

146. Tali Sharot, "The Optimism Bias," *Time,* May 28, 2011, http://www.
time.com/time/health/article/0,8599,2074067,00.html#ixzz1cZLsINc8.

147. Stockdale did everything in his power to lift the morale and prolong the
lives of his fellow prisoners. He created a tapping code so they could
communicate with each other. He developed a milestone system that
helped them deal with torture. And he sent intelligence information to
his wife, hidden in the seemingly innocent letters he wrote.

148. Chet McDoniel, *I'm Not Broken: You Don't Need Arms to Be Happy*
(CreateSpace, 2009).

149. http://chetmcdoniel.com/ (Is there a specific article to cite?)

150. Price Pritchett, *Hard Optimism: How to Succeed in a World Where
Positive Wins* (New York: McGraw-Hill, 2007), 73.

151. Paul, "Optimism and Pessimism."

152. Psychologists tell us that pessimism is an ego-protection strategy that
prevents us from absorbing too big a blow to our self-image or self-
esteem should things not work out as we wished they would. In fact,

studies show that pessimism can help us see things more accurately, actually increasing our perception of danger, sensitizing us to potential problems, and protecting us in high risk situations.

153. Paul, "Optimism and Pessimism."

154. Walter Wink, *The Powers That Be: A Theology for a New Millimium* (New York: Doubleday, 1999), 185–86.

155. Ibid., 186.

156. James McGregor Burns, *Transforming Leadership: A New Pursuit of Happiness* (New York: Grove Press, 2003), 239.

157. Adapted from a Dominican folktale presented in William Bennett's book, *Virtues of Leadership*.

158. David Meyer. http://www.davidmyers.org/davidmyers/assets/Hum.Theol.Meets.Psych.pdf

159. Barry Schlenker. Egocentric Perceptions in Cooperative Groups: A Conceptualization and Research review," Final Report, Office of Naval Research Grant NR 170-797, 1976); Barry Schlenker and R. Miller, "Egocentrism in Group; Self –serving Biases or Logical Information Processing? *Journal of Personality and Social Psychology*, 35 (1977b), 755-764; and Barry Schlenker and R. Miller, "Group Cohesiveness as a Determinant of Egocentric Perceptions in Cooperative Groups," *Human Relations*, 30 (1977a), 1039-1055.

160. In terms of positive psychology, self-control is often used interchangeably with self-regulation, which is the process of exerting control over oneself in order to achieve goals or meet standards. Self regulating individuals are able to control instinctive responses such as aggression and impulsivity, responding instead according to pre-conceived standards of behavior.

161. In modern psychological terms, a person who is able to exercise self-control is seen as possessing an internal locus of control and experiences the positive outcomes such an orientation can produce. In effect, he or she is in control rather than helpless.

162. James Q. Wilson, one of the foremost modern scholars on the subject of cultivating virtues, has written that having good character means at least two things: empathy and self-control. Empathy is the ability to take into account the rights, needs, and feelings of others. Self-control is the practice of deferred gratification or being more concerned with the long-term impact of conduct than with the "here and now."

163. On May 26, 1983, People Express began non-stop service from Newark to London's Gatwick Airport with a leased Boeing 747-227B previously operated by Braniff International Airways. In 1985, People Express bought out Denver-based Frontier Airlines. The combined company

became the <u>United States'</u> fifth largest airline, with flights to most major U.S. cities, as well as an additional transatlantic route to <u>Brussels</u>. During this period, People Express also purchased Midwest commuter carrier <u>Britt Airways</u> and <u>Provincetown-Boston Airlines</u> (PBA), a regional airline with route networks in New England and Florida.

164. The failed integration and enormous debt stretched People Express too far, and in June, 1986, the company announced it was working with an investment bank to seek buyers for part, or all, of the airline. A deal to sell Frontier off to <u>United Airlines</u> fell through due to the inability of United to agree to terms with its unions on how to incorporate Frontier's staff, leading People Express management to cease Frontier's operations and file the subsidiary for bankruptcy protection. In the end, People Express was forced to sell itself entirely to <u>Texas Air Corporation</u> for roughly $125 million in cash, notes, and assumed debt. People Express ceased to exist as a carrier on February 1, 1987, when its operations were merged into the operations of <u>Continental Airlines</u>, another Texas Air subsidiary, under a joint marketing agreement.

165. Ray Silverstein. Is Your Ego Becoming a Liability? The best leaders know how to check their ego at the door. *Entrepreneur.* July 26, 2010. Viewed at http://www.entrepreneur.com/article/207642

166. Such a positive approach to leadership reflects a decades-old tension between two competing theories of leadership, known as Theory X and Theory Y. Originally articulated by Douglas McGregor at MIT's Sloan School of Management in the 1960's, the theory differentiates between how people are perceived in an organization.

167. Peterson, C., & Seligman, M.E.P. *Character Strengths and Virtues: A Handbook and Classification* (New York: Oxford/American Psychological Association. 2004).

168. Shackleton was on Scott's first unsuccessful voyage to reach the South Pole and made a return voyage that came within 97 miles of its intended goal. His participation in this famed voyage brought him international acclaim and a British Knighthood.

169. Emmons, R. A., and M. E. McCullough. Counting Blessings versus Burdens: Experimental Studies of Gratitude and Subjective Well Being in Daily Life. *Journal of Personality and Social psychology*, 84 (2003): 377-389

170. McCullough, M. E., Emmons, R. A., & Tsang, J. (2002). The grateful disposition: A conceptual and empirical topography. *Journal of Personality and Social Psychology, 82*, 112-127. Wood, A. M., Joseph, S., & Maltby, J. (2008). <u>Gratitude uniquely predicts satisfaction with life: Incremental validity above the domains and facets of the Five Factor Model.</u> *Personality and Individual Differences, 45*, 49-54.

171. Preliminary theories on the nuts-and-bolts physiology behind gratitude point scientists to the left prefrontal cortex of the brain, which is also associated with positive emotions like love and compassion.

172. Paul Goldman, "Delivering Hope in South Africa," *Huffington Post*, April 5, 2008, http://www.huffingtonpost.com/paula-goldman/ delivering-hope-in-south_b_95142.html.

173. As Simone repeatedly discovered, the weeks and months just before and after birth are an ideal time for intervention. New mothers are more willing to access medical and psychological care, and the support provided can lay the foundation for healthy families for decades to come.

174. To learn more about PMHP or donate to their cause, please visit http:// www.pmhp.za.org/.

175. Goldman, "Delivering Hope."

176. Few people realize that to bless literally means "to speak well of."

177. Ruth Davidhizar. (2005). "The Benefits of Saying Thank You for the Ordinary Rather than the Extraordinary." *Journal of Practical Nursing*, 55, 27-30.

178. Kim Cameron. (2008). *Positive Leadership*. San Francisco: Berret-Koehler Publishers, Inc.

179. http://www.answers.com/topic/gratitude

180. Simmel, Georg. (1950). *The Sociology of Georg Simmel.* Glencoe, IL: Free Press. P. 388

181. P. 242

182. As the late President John F. Kennedy once said, "As we express our gratitude, we must never forget that the highest appreciation is not to utter words, but to live by them

183. John C. Kunich and Richard I. Lester, "Profile of a Leader: The Wallenberg Effect," (white paper, March 29, 2002).

184. Ibid.

185. Wallenberg was recommended for this mission by Koloman Lauer, a business partner who was involved with the new War Refugee Board. Lauer believed Raoul possessed the proper combination of dedication, skill, and courage, despite his youth and inexperience, to pull off such a bold endeavor.

186. Ibid.

187. Kati Marton, *Wallenberg: Missing Hero* (New York: Random House, 1982) 110–11.

188. John Bierman, *Righteous Gentile: The Story of Raoul Wallenberg, Missing Hero of the Holocaust* (New York: Viking Press, 1981), 80. Emphasis added.

189. Kunich and Lester, "The Wallenberg Effect."

190. Ibid.

191. Ibid.

192. Ibid.

193. Bierman, *Righteous Gentile*. Emphasis added.

194. *Corporate Leadership Council*, (March 31 2008); available from https://www.clc.executiveboard.com.

195. Ibid.

196. Jedd Medefind and Erik Lokkesmoe, *The Revolutionary Communicator: Seven Principles Jesus Lived to Impact, Connect and Lead* (Lake Mary, FL: Relevant Books, 2004), 85.

197. Tim Elmore, *Habitudes: Leadership Habits and Attitudes* (Atlanta: Growing Leaders, Inc., 2004), 2.

198. This summary of Adolph Hitler was influenced and adapted from Tim Elmore's superb series, "Habitudes."

199. Ibid.

200. Frank J. Snyder, Samuel Kucinich, Alan Acock, Isaac J. Washburn, Brian R. Flay, "Improving Elementary School Quality through the Use of a Social-Emotional and Character Development Program: A Matched-Pair, Cluster Randomized, Controlled Trial in Hawaii," *Journal of School Science* 82, no. 1 (2012): 11. doi: 10.1111/j.1746-1561.2011.00662.x.

201. Ibid.

202. "Key to School Improvement: Reading, Writing, Arithmetic... and Character?," *Science Daily*, December 30, 2011, http://www.sciencedaily.com/releases/2011/12/111230134836.htm.

203. Michael D. Wyly, "In Praise of Mavericks: A True Professional Will Strive to Do Something, Not Be Someone," *Armed Forces Journal* (July 2008).

204. During the early 1960s, Boyd, together with a civilian mathematician named Thomas Christie, created the Energy-Maneuverability, or E-M, theory of aerial combat still in use today. Legend has it Boyd "stole" the computer time to do the millions of calculations necessary to prove the theory, which became the world standard for the design of fighter planes.

205. Wyly, "In Praise of Mavericks."

206. Ibid., 2.

207. Boyd is credited for largely developing the strategy for the invasion of Iraq in the first Gulf War. In a letter to the editor of *Inside the Pentagon*, former commandant of the Marine Corps General Charles C. Krulak is quoted as saying, "The Iraqi army collapsed morally and intellectually under the onslaught of American and Coalition forces. John Boyd was an architect of that victory as surely as if he'd commanded a fighter wing or a maneuver division in the desert." See Grant Tedrick Hammond, *The Mind of War: John Boyd and American Security* (Washington, DC: Smithsonian Institution Press, 2001), 3.

208. Ibid.

209. Marcus Buckingham and Curt Coffman, *First, Break All the Rules: What the World's Greatest Managers Do Differently* (New York: Simon and Schuster, 1999).

210. "Rosa Parks: The Woman Who Changed a Nation," interview by Kira Albin, 1996, www.grandtimes.com/rosa.html.

211. William Jennings Bryan, "Cross of Gold," (speech, Democratic National Convention, Chicago, July 9, 1896). The issue was whether to endorse the free coinage of silver at a ratio of 16 to 1, silver to gold. (This inflationary measure would have increased the amount of money in circulation and aided cash-poor and debt-burdened farmers.) After speeches on the subject by several US Senators, Bryan rose to speak. The thirty-six-year-old former Congressman from Nebraska aspired to be the Democratic nominee for president, and he had been skillfully, but quietly, building support for himself among the delegates. His dramatic speaking style and rhetoric roused the crowd to a frenzy. The response, wrote one reporter, "came like one great burst of artillery." Men and women screamed and waved their hats and canes. "Some," wrote another reporter, "like demented things, divested themselves of their coats and flung them high in the air." The next day the convention nominated Bryan for president on the fifth ballot. The full text of William Jennings Bryan's speech can be found at http://historymatters. gmu.edu/d/5354.

212. Michael Josephson, "What Will Matter," *What Will Matter* (blog), http://whatwillmatter.com/about/the-poem/.

213. Adapted story. See Jessica Haberkern, "The Embrace of Extraordinary Love," *InTouch*, April 2012, http://www.intouch.org/magazine/content/topic/the_embrace_of_extraordinary_love.

214. Please go to http://www.amazima.org/ to learn more about Katie's work or to donate to her cause.

215. Adapted story. See Jessica Haberkern, "The Embrace of Extraordinary Love," *In Touch*, April 2012, http://www.intouch.org/magazine/content/topic/the_embrace_of_extraordinary_love, 26.

216. Ibid., 28.

217. J. T. Fisher, as quoted in Josh McDowell, *More than a Carpenter* (Colorado Springs: Living Books, 1987), 32.

218. Ronald Reagan's Inaugural Address, January 20, 1981, quoted in George Grant's *The American Patriot's Handbook: The Writings, History, and Spirit of a Free Nation* (Naperville, IL: Cumberland House, 2009), 385–386.

219. Ibid., 386.

220. Credit for alerting me to this quote goes to pastor and author, Mark Batterson.

CPSIA information can be obtained at www.ICGtesting.com
Printed in the USA
BVOW070932110413

317935BV00002B/162/P